THE CANNON KING'S DAUGHTER

THE CANNON
KING'S DAUGHTER

Banished from a Dynasty The True, Untold Story of Engelbertha Krupp

DAVID G. STROEBEL

For information regarding permission, write to: David G. Stroebel, c/o Webster Avenue Writers, LLC, 2 Naomi Road, Ocean, New Jersey, 07712.

Stroebel, David. *The Cannon Kings Daughter: Banished from a dynasty, the true, untold story of Engelbertha Krupp.* North Carolina: CreateSpace, 2010.

David G. Stroebel
Visit my website at www.davidstroebel.com

Printed in the United States of America

ISBN- 9780615465289
ISBN: 0615465285

CONTENTS

ILLUSTRATIONS

GLOSSARY

A.G. (aktiengesellschaft)	Corporation
Kunstmaler und Hofphotograph	Painter and Court Photographer
Kruppianer	Krupp worker
Leiter Presse- und Offentlichkeitsarbeit	Head of Press and Public Relations
Lex Krupp	Hitler's Krupp decree
Marktkirche	Market Church in Essen
Prokura	Management committee
Roter-Adler-Orden,	Order of the Eagle, Fourth Class
Schloss Sigmaringen	Castle Sigmaringen
Stammhaus	Ancestral home of Alfred Krupp
St. Johann's	Catholic Church in Sigmaringen
Villa Hugel	Krupp 300-room castle in Essen overlooking the Ruhr River

The Cannon King's Daughter

For
Caroline Marchuck, Charles M. Stroebele and Theodore J. Beebe Sr. this book is
dedicated. Their revelations and photographs have made this story possible.

PROLOGUE

In Germany, it was accepted knowledge that Alfred and Bertha Krupp had only one child—Friedrich Krupp. Strong and unmistakable evidence has revealed that they had a second child, a daughter they named Engelbertha, who was banished for defying orders not to marry a poor, Catholic shoemaker named John Joseph Stroebele who was employed at the Krupp's Villa Hugel Estate in Essen. Centuries-old revelations, documents, and photographs passed down through five generations of the New York and New Jersey Stroebele family reveal intriguing details of Engelbertha Krupp, Germany's dethroned Cannon Queen who chose love over a family dynasty's wealth and was banished forever.

Chapter 1

ESSEN AND KRUPP

The city of Essen is situated in the central-most part of the German state of North Rhine-Westphalia and sits near the Ruhr River. The city's roots go back to approximately the year 845, when St. Alfred (800-874) established an Abbey for women known in the present day as the center of Essen. It was in the year 1587 that the first Krupp, Arndt Krupp, first surfaced here. He is documented as being a member of the Merchant's Guild of Essen.[1] A trader, Arndt arrived in Essen just after much of the city's population was compelled to flee by the pandemic plague that swept through it. Exhibiting the fledgling traits of the family's trademark opportunistic spirit, he purchased many of the homes of those who had fled at well below market value.[2] When the plague was eradicated, the homes regained their original value and Krupp found himself with a substantial windfall and became one of the wealthiest men in Essen. It was here that the family's fortune began to proliferate. Arndt, a man to whom history was invariably kind, painting him as a philanthropic, fair and honest politician, would not live long enough to see the scope of his impact two hundred years later.[3]

The Thirty-Years War was fought from the years 1618-1648. It was a religious war that pitted the minority Catholics against the more dominant Protestants and proved that the two factions could not prosper. Princess-Abbess Maria Clara Von Spaur-Pflaum und Valor, led the city's Catholic

Spaniards in an uprising against Essen in an effort to force the city into accepting counter-reformation. As it stood, present rulers of Germany's 225 states could choose the religion to which their state would adhere and show reverence. A *re-Catholicization law* was passed by Essen's government in 1624 that severely limited Catholics from attending church. The Thirty-Years War was one of the most destructive wars ever fought in Germany.

The emergence of the Krupp family in Essen was of strategic importance. The family established its very first iron forge in 1800 on a stream in Essen.[4] In 1807 Friedrich Krupp (1787-1826) was charged with its management by his mother, Helene Amalie Ascherfeld Krupp. Helene had managed through her lifetime to considerably grow the family's fortune, acquiring a prosperous mill and shares in at least four local coal mines in addition to their already widespread empire.[5]

Just nineteen years of age, Friedrich lacked the vision, leadership, and experience to guide the family business to greener pastures. As a result, the business failed, forcing Helene to sell. Despite the difficulties of this setback, Friedrich didn't part from his ways, and continued to squander the family fortune. For some reason, upon her death in 1810, Helene nevertheless bequeathed the family's remaining wealth to him. This decision cost the family dearly and derailed all that Friedrich's forbearers had established thus far.

Empowered with a large sum of cash, Friedrich set out to learn the secret of cast (crucible) steel and founded the Krupp Gusstahlfabrik (cast steel works) in 1811.[6] Underestimating the enormity of this undertaking, he discovered that a mill and foundry was required to power the facility, and before long was allocating very large sums of time and money toward this endeavor. Eventually he neglected all other family business and, hemorrhaging cash, they failed one by one. In 1816, Friedrich finally produced his first batch of smelted steel, however, he would soon die at the young age of thirty-nine.

Friedrich's widow was left to take on the family, placing the bulk of the responsibility on her fourteen-year-old son, Alfred—my great-great-grandfather. Alfred viewed his newfound responsibility as little more than a burden. He believed his father was a failure and expressed these feelings.[7] The sight of his father withering away in his bed filled him with disgust and frustration.[8]

Nevertheless, he had forever left school to pick up the pieces of his father's tarnished legacy. Alfred would have to deal with his father's 15 years of fruitless labor that generated sales barely sufficient for payroll thereby forcing the family into a life of extreme frugality.

Alfred's first break came in 1841, when he invented the spoon-roller.[9] Profits from this revolutionary invention enabled him to expand his factory so he could begin the important undertaking of casting steel blocks. Six years later, Alfred produced his very first six-pounder cannon made exclusively of his own cast-steel and proudly displayed it in France at the Great Exhibition of 1851, along with a flawless solid steel ingot weighing one ton.[10] At the time, two thousand pounds was double the amount ever cast by anyone who came before him. Alfred became a huge sensation in the engineering world and the Krupp brand rapidly flourished.

The company created the cannons used to obliterate Napoleon's Army in Sedan, France during the Franco-Prussian War, easily handing a victory to Prussia.[11] His factories and fortune continued to expand, and he became the family savior, enabling the continued growth of the 400-year-old family dynasty we know today.

With wealth comes power. This was evident within the city during the early years of Krupp's success. Alfred created the first subsidized housing known as Krupp Colonies, for his employees he called, "Kruppianer." The housing extended to workers and families and included schools, hospitals, and parks. Alfred also created widow and orphan insurance benefits for workers who died or suffered serious illness.[12]

It is true that Alfred sought to control all aspects of his workers' lives. [13] He went to extreme measures to ensure he had this, demanding loyalty oaths from them, demanding permission slips from supervisors for bathroom breaks, making them sign promises that they wouldn't get involved in political affairs, etc.[14] In reality, Alfred was nothing like the kind, generous philanthropist that German history suggests. He knew the only way to exercise control over his workers was to entice them with lavish benefits. He controlled his family in the same way. If they resisted control, they immediately became a threat to him. His wife, Bertha, found this out when she left him. Privately he leveraged every weapon at his disposal to assassinate her character within his own mind, but keeping his thoughts private. He expressed his dissatisfaction with her by turning her suites at Villa Hugel into storerooms.[15] Strict social customs of the time forbade the public airing of family business, so little is known about the event to those outside the immediate family.

The power Alfred wielded over Essen was seen and felt throughout the city by its inhabitants. He donated copious amounts of money to the Protestant Church of Essen so they could construct new churches to satisfy the ever-growing population of Essen's churchgoers.[16] Parishioners would find all the bibles and crosses inscribed with the words, "personal property of Krupp."[17] This was done to demonstrate that were it not for Alfred's generosity, the church would have surely gone bankrupt. This was a questionable act considering the man was described as a militant atheist.[18] This was not an act of kindness, but a demonstration of power. This power over the church was soon used in an evil and unforgiving way when it is believed that Alfred had his daughter's baptism and other records wiped clean from church records and banished her from the life she had been given. This secret penetrated the highest level of the church and would remain hidden for over 135 years.

Alfred and Bertha are said to have had their son, Friedrich, baptized on February 17, 1854, in a church in Essen formerly known as St. Gertrude's Church. Today it is known as the Market Church and was the only church in that area during that time, according to officials at the Protestant Church of Essen. During his early childhood years, Friedrich (known as, "Fritz,") was a delicate and ill child. Friedrich was so often ill that his father deliberated for quite some time over whether to disinherit him.[19] Alfred thought that setting him up as a gentleman farmer would better serve the family and the Krupp brand. But that meant that the firm would be sacrificed to the state with no heir to will it to—or maybe not as he indirectly tells us he has an heiress aside from Fritz, and she is Engelbertha. To Alfred's delight, when Friedrich reached adolescence, his health improved. No longer was Alfred thinking of disowning him.[20]

Bertha and Alfred's marriage was certainly under a great amount of strain from the beginning from Alfred's dominance and peculiar behaviors. They increasingly fought whenever they were together. Alfred, known to be a note-writing addict, would pen Bertha notes after these quarrels as a substitute for shortcomings in his ability to orally communicate with her. Alfred's dominance increased over Friedrich the next few years, and their relationship could perhaps best be characterized as a competition for his favor between he and his wife, Bertha.[21] That was Alfred's way and nothing or nobody could change it. Alfred had a genuine stake in the way Friedrich developed as a young man, as he was to eventually inherit the business and emulate his father's success. Friedrich was most probably afraid of his father, due in large part to his fits of rage and frequent temper outbursts.[22] He was not able to finish his normal schooling, as his father ordered him to withdraw for apparently illogical and selfish reasons.[23] Friedrich was his only son, and he wanted as much time with him as possible. He also wanted to keep the boy away from his mother as often as he possibly could. Why is a mystery only Alfred could answer. Ultimately this power play proved futile—a stunning defeat for Alfred given his track record in the control department.

To illustrate how far Friedrich was willing to go to get away from his father, he complied with Prussian Military Conscription Law requiring military service for men around the year 1870.[24] Being careful not to show his father that his entering the Prussian Army was intentional, he cited law and love for his country as reasons for joining the Prussian Officer Corps. Alfred looked favorably on the decision and would spare the violent outbursts. Unfortunately, for Friedrich, after being assigned to the Third Baden Dragoons, and after being only partially indoctrinated, he was discharged for failure to meet Prussian military physical standards.[25] He was found to be shortsighted, overweight, lethargic, and suffering from asthma.[26] Upon his discharge, Friedrich was greeted by a grinning Alfred who was overjoyed that his son was back at his side, never knowing that his son was inches from escaping his iron rule. Friedrich was notably angry that his only chance to escape his life had been taken from him.[27] Upon Alfred's death from a heart attack on July 14, 1887, Friedrich inherited the company and the family fortune, running the business with more success and efficiency than anyone who came before him. This was due in large part to his philanthropic and charitable nature. Under his watch,

Fried. Krupp became a global force in business, developing Hiram Maxim's machine-gun and building Rudolf Diesel's famous diesel engine.[28] One of the most notable programs was the infamous and deadly German U-boat Program that quietly and unmercifully hunted and sunk civilian passenger ships, merchant ships, fishing boats, supply vessels, and troop transports during World War II.[29] These programs were game changers and Friedrich was at the helm, in much the same way his father was when he made the first cannon of crucible steel that defeated Napoleon's Army.

Friedrich married Margarete von Ende. The couple had two daughters, one named Bertha (1886-1957) the other Barbara (1887-1972).[30] When Friedrich was photographed allegedly having sex with underage boys in a hotel in Capri in 1902, the scandal was said to be so great that he suffered a stroke and died.[31] When his immediate family and close friends were told they could not see his body, rumors spread that he committed suicide, possibly suggesting that his head or face were horribly disfigured from a gunshot blast.[32] According to the Stamford Stroke Center, a one-time stressful event such as Friedrich's outing will rarely cause a stroke.[33] However, a long-term stressful event that goes unresolved will.[34] Applying today's medical technology to Friedrich's death, it is difficult to accept the conclusion that the incident was responsible for his death. We must then consider two other possibilities: suicide or falsification of his death to salvage the company's reputation.

Logistically speaking, the legal guardian of his body (whoever that was) would have wanted his family to see his body out of respect for them as the richest family in Germany. One person was likely responsible for barring the immediate family from viewing the body. In 1902 the most powerful force in Prussia, Emperor Wilhelm II could enforce such an order. There was a mysterious absence of protest from within the Krupp family when the order was issued. It is not far-fetched to assume that he gave—and enforced the order. With Friedrich's death went the last Krupp namesake. He had two daughters and they eventually took on the names of their husbands. By law in Germany, women were not permitted to operate family businesses, but they could inherit them. Instead of losing the company, Emperor Wilhelm II orchestrated an arranged marriage between Bertha Krupp and Gustav von Bohlen und Halbach that would allow Bertha to inherit the company, but allowed her husband, Gustav to run every aspect of it.[35] By doing this, Emperor Wilhelm II ensured the survival of the vast company that would eventually supply Germany with superior ammunition and armaments for two world wars. In 1918 the allies named Gustav a war criminal and were set to bring him to a military tribunal, but the tribunals never materialized.[36] When Gustav could no longer effectively run the company in 1943, Hitler approved passage of the Lex Krupp decree, approving the transfer of all Bertha Krupp's stock to her eldest son, Alfried, giving him complete ownership.[37]

Alfried led the company through the second half of World War II. He conscripted tens of thousands of Jews from Auschwitz Concentration Camp near Krakow, Poland to work in the factories where a vast majority of them would face a horrible death.[38] Between 1,000 and 8,000 infants were separated from their horrified and distraught mothers and placed in separate isolated infirmaries—Buschmannshof/Voerde-West where they all died of malnutrition, disease, and neglect.[39] None of these innocent young souls survived captivity there. Children and elderly men were expected to labor intensively far, far beyond their physical capabilities, while being supplied with criminally meager and inadequate food rations and basic sanitary care.[40]

When the war ended, Alfried Krupp was arrested on the grounds of Villa Hugel and convicted at the Nuremberg Tribunals. During the trials, he displayed the same disinterested and unemotional demeanor as he had throughout the committal of his crimes against humanity.[41] His response to the legal predicament in which he found himself was to hire very large numbers of unscrupulous lawyers whose main interests were seeing that Alfried was acquitted and the Krupp name restored. On sentencing day, he was ordered to serve 12 years for using forced slave labor in Krupp factories. He was released on clemency by John J. McCloy, High Commissioner of the American zone of occupation on January 31, 1951.[42]

Ironically, serving as warden in the same Nuremburg Prison where Alfried and other top Nazi war criminals were housed during the trials was his

American cousin, US Army First Lieutenant Otto "Dave" Stroebel of Jersey City, New Jersey.[43] It is unknown, if at all, how many times their paths crossed during their respective tenures. Otto D. Stroebel died in 1996. His wife, Arlaine Robb, said he never spoke much about the war.[44] He was part of that greatest generation that rarely spoke of their service during World War II.

Chapter 2

PASSENGER 974

It is early March 1883. A woman hurries aboard a Holland-America German passenger ship, the SS *Westphalia,* at the Port of Hamburg with three bags and her three young children. She's traveled almost four hundred miles— probably by train and has prepared herself for the second leg of her long journey. She is weary, yet determined to make it to America, and her husband who awaits her arrival three thousand miles across the Atlantic. Careful not to draw attention to herself or children, she offers four second-class tickets to the ship's personnel who then scribble her name onto the passenger list. She is Passenger number 974, and she is about to leave the only home she's known for the past 32 years.[1] "Vorname?" asks the Stewart (first name). "Engelbertha," she replies. He probes her for her last name. "Nachname?" "Stroebele" she replies. "Ursprungsland?" continues the Stewart, asking for her country of origin. "Prussia," she replies. "Bestimmungsort?" (destination). "New York City." He glances into the eyes of the thirty-two-year-old wife and mother. He goes about his business and Engelbertha moves along. She scurries with her children reminding herself not to intermingle with the other passengers through fear of being robbed of her belongings, which according to some estimates are worth around $200,000—believed to be mostly diamonds which are lighter to carry than gold and silver coins given to her by her father Alfred Krupp. These by the way are 1883 dollars. They are most-likely sewn into hers and her children's clothing—including in my 11-month-old grandfather's clothing. The journey from Hamburg to New York takes approximately 14 days, during which time Engelbertha remains in her cabin, apart from letting her children go to the bathroom reserved for first and second-class cabins. She allows no one to enter their cabin, nor does she befriend anyone on the ship. She is careful to leave no evidence of her presence onboard. The massive frame of the *Westphalia* quietly slips into New York Harbor. For Engelbertha, it was a fresh start and relief that she was beyond the reach of her tormented past in Essen. On March 27, 1883, the *Westphalia* delivered her secret cargo to Castle Garden Immigration Center in Lower Manhattan, New York City making it an unwitting accomplice in one of the most historic getaways in German history.[2] For nearly two weeks in March 1883 the *Westphalia* quietly carried Engelbertha and her three children across the frigid waters to their new home in America. Nobody knew her, if they had, she might have been everybody's friend. Engelbertha's husband, John Joseph Stroebele had left the small apartment they'd shared with their children in the picturesque town of Sigmaringen, nestled in the farmland of southeast Germany in Hohenzollern, Prussia, known today as the German state of Baden-Wurttemberg. John had left nearly four months earlier for the United States to search for a new home for his family. Having set sail alone from the Port of Antwerp on SS *Zeeland*, he arrived at Castle Garden on December 5, 1882.[3]

Of the three possible ports of embarkation, he could have chosen Hamburg, Antwerp, or Le Havre in France. The thirty-seven-year-old husband and Master Shoemaker chose the port closest to his home and became passenger 163 on the vessel sailing from Antwerp.[4] He traveled very light in Steerage, suggesting that Engelbertha transported the family fortune. Steerage on these ships was often a dirty, disease-ridden place, where one could easily be killed and robbed of their life savings.

John and Engelbertha met at a very troubled time in her life. Her relationship with her father had been strained to the point of no return and was now a cold, distant thing kept alive only by blood-ties. German men were traditionally chauvinists. If an industrialist like Alfred Krupp had sired a girl, there was a good chance she'd be the subject of scorn throughout her life. Compared to her brother, Friedrich, Engelbertha was not a best fit to inherit the Krupp helm due to her gender.

It is probable that John Stroebele began his employment as a Bootblack in the boot maker's shop at Villa Hugel between 1871 and 1873 after serving in the Franco-Prussian War. Alfred had employed some 3,000 new workers since July 1871 just two months after the Franco-Prussian War had ended.[5] Could John Stroebele had been one of those 3,000 new workers? It is fact that John Stroebele was living in Mengen, Baden-Wurttemberg, prior to him serving in the Franco-Prussian War. We know this because his name appears on a German baptism record for his nephew, Eugene John Kromer on June 12, 1870, at St. John's Catholic Church in Sigmaringen.[6] For some reason, he chose to travel to, or was discharged from the Prussian Army where he initially entered service. It is believed that after beginning a friendship that blossomed into love, Engelbertha likely went to her mother with the joyous news that she found real love and chance to escape the domineering hold of her father.

Bertha Krupp was a mother who gave the impression that she advocated women's rights; this trait was likely passed to her daughter and nourished on a daily basis. Engelbertha already had her mind made up before news of her engagement reached her father. This couldn't have left Alfred very happy. This kind of disobedience would not be tolerated. After all, this was the same man who, after visiting son Friedrich's newborn baby girl, was quoted as saying, "all children are vermin."[7]

This father wanted no part of dispensing the love and attention that every young girl craves from a father. It is her quest to find a loving family life that brings her to John Stroebele, the relatively poor but devoted son of a Mengen schoolteacher.[8] One could only imagine the scene of Alfred learning of his daughter's newfound love. Engelbertha knew to expect immediate and uncontrollable rage, but stood her ground. One's thoughts go to disinheritance—by this time a common practice in the Krupp dynasty—among many of the other punishments that were likely doled out by the patriarch.

What must have been paramount in Alfred's mind in this state was the use of brute force in an effort to get Engelbertha to break the engagement.

This would also, more than likely, lead to an arranged marriage to a more suitable, or gifted business-minded life partner; one that would know what to do with the enormous wealth he would inherit in the wake of Germany's anti-feminist laws.

Like her brother, Friedrich, Engelbertha was the complete antithesis of her raging, eccentric and distant father. She wanted no part of the Krupp money or the name. The only thing she really ever shared with her father was her nose and mouth. It's as if something beyond the natural world willed her to have her mother's compassionate and knowing eyes. Her face is shown exhibiting strong and unmistakable characteristics of both parents in a family photograph taken in 1868-69.[9]

One of the most unfortunate—and perhaps telling things about the Krupp story is that there are more stories about their business skills than their personal lives; the flesh-and-blood of the dynasty. The rags-to-riches, triumph-over-tragedy stories have been the historical party line since the first words about this family were written. Their children, most specifically Engelbertha, are conveniently absent from an overwhelming majority of their history—a puzzling and unfortunate fact. However, there is a photograph circulating, the caption of which commonly appears as *Krupp family with friends*. If one gets a chance to look even briefly at the photograph, they will certainly notice a beautiful young woman standing out. She is sitting to Bertha's right. The caption says the young woman's name is Clara Bruch.[10] A cursory glance at the young woman will illustrate an unavoidable resemblance to Bertha and Alfred Krupp. Why are there not more photos like this one? Did Alfred order all of the pictures that showed his pariah daughter to be destroyed? Could this photo have been hidden away by Bertha, or perhaps a sympathetic house-maid? The simple answer is that only one family photograph exists today when there should be dozens, even hundreds.

Only a handful of family photographs of Alfred and his family have been made available for public view. That does not imply there were many more, just that only a handful have been viewed. They could not have been the result of the allied serial bombings during World War II that devastated Germany. It is a fact that all the Krupp archives were safely transported to an alternate location during the war to ensure their survival.[11] Luckily, for the Krupp family, their records remained intact. However, unlucky for them, they were seized by the allied forces as a war-prize and kept from the family for nine long years.[12] It's important to note that no records or photograph were destroyed during that time. However, there were no reports of such acts by allied troops when they came upon the archives during the American Ninth Army's capture of Essen.

What does one do if they're the daughter of the, "Cannon King," Alfred Krupp and married to a shoemaker in southern Germany with the wish to remain inconspicuous? Perhaps you use an assumed name for yourself and to ensure your safety in an effort to fool the church into marrying you, while you keep your true identity a secret. That's exactly what is believed Engelbertha did. If she had disclosed to the priest at St. John's Catholic Church in Sigmaringen that her Krupp family was Protestant she would have been unable to marry in the Catholic Church without first communicating that fact, and agreeing in writing to raise her children as Catholics. Engelbertha would have also had to explain their situation, why she was unmarried, three months pregnant, and using an assumed name. We can answer that easily for her: she was the daughter of Alfred and Bertha Krupp.

Engelbertha's situation required closer examination. How did she come to be at such odds with her father? It can be argued that she chose to cut herself off from her family and her inheritance voluntarily that may be only half true. Caroline Marchuck has stated that the story of Engelbertha Krupp and John Stroebele was passed down through her grandfather Adolph Stroebele of Secaucus, New Jersey was that Alfred Krupp told his daughter, "Never darken my door again," after giving her a very large sum of money to immigrate to America with.[13] That implies that Engelbertha returned to Villa Hugel for the money and that she and John were broke. Why then did she ask for more of the money from which she'd spent the last few years running from?

We can conclude from the story and the documentation of her return, that she didn't voluntarily remove herself from the family. It could have been her father for her failure to obey his command to end her relationship with John Stroebele. Perhaps when she stood up to Alfred, knowing that her mother would back her decision and force Alfred into submission. We don't know for sure this ever happened. We do know however, that Bertha stayed with Alfred until 1882, after which time she moved out of Villa Hugel and away from Alfred forever.[14] What you do not see is also apparent. She didn't back her daughter and for that, Engelbertha most likely never forgave her mother. Bertha chose status and wealth that the Krupp name commanded over her own daughter.

Chapter 3

THE FAMILY SECRET

While visiting my eighty-five-year-old father in his home at the Jersey Shore in March 2007 he received a call from his sister, seventy-eight-year-old Dorothy Borchers. Our side of the family dropped the last, "e," at the end of our last name long ago. I always enjoyed hearing from my aunt Dorothy through the years. She was the youngest of 13 children born to Otto and Julia Stroebel, who grew up on Webster Avenue in the heights section of Jersey City. She called to deliver sad news that their sister—Aunt Gloria Bekker—died after spending the past 42 years in a nursing home due to a devastating car accident in 1966. The cause of death is breast cancer.

Aunt Gloria was running some errands when another car drove through an intersection and caused an accident that would forever change the lives of her family. My father had eleven siblings growing up (another—Robert, died at age 17 months), but due to various circumstances, fell out of contact with most of them. Having so many uncles and aunts out there while growing up was a sore spot for us, having only met very few of them. I was always curious as to whether or not they actually wanted to see us. I felt particularly guilty about my Aunt Gloria; the car accident basically robbed her of her life and I never made an attempt to make the trip to visit her. During the funeral for my grandmother Julia Anne Stroebel in 1986, all my relatives were whispering to one another in inquiry regarding the presence of my Uncle Dave. Would he show for the funeral? His attendance didn't seem likely. As we all walked to the grave someone said, "There's Dave." Uncle Dave did come to say a final farewell to his mother. When my father called out to him, he walked away from us quickly toward his car in the distance. He had challenges in his life and from the war that the rest of the family couldn't understand, challenges that kept him away from those who loved him. This occasion was the closest I came to meeting my namesake.

I saw my Aunt Dorothy the most out of all my relatives since we both skated at the same ice-rink in Totowa where I took skating lessons. In spite of my extended family's absence from my childhood and adult life, when Aunt Gloria had died, it changed the way I thought about the relatives I had never known. I knew that if I didn't take the initiative to start writing things down and asking questions about my family, I would be lost for information when all of them were gone. I also wanted my children to know who their relatives were. I remembered not long ago seeing a commercial on television regarding a popular genealogy web site called Ancestry.com. The next day I went on the Internet and began using it to build my family tree. I was fortunate to know the names of all my aunts and uncles as well as those of my grandparents. After I made some calls to my father and Aunt Dorothy, I had all the information I needed. I found Ancestry.com especially helpful because the access they grant to Census reports and other government documents such as war draft cards. It also automatically searches other member's family trees for matches to my family tree.

After completing my family tree, I started to wonder who my great-grandparents were. I remember my father saying that his grandfather's name was John and that he lived on Palisade Avenue in Jersey City. I soon found John and Bertha (Engelbertha) Stroebele on a 1900 Census report living at 1 Patterson Plank Road in Jersey City.[1] They had three sons living with them named John, Adolph, and Otto (my grandfather). More searching revealed John and Engelbertha's name on a 1910 Census, the very last time Engelbertha's name would appear on a Census.[2] They'd emigrated three years too late to be counted on the 1880 Census report and the 1890 count had perished in a fire in Washington, D.C. To make a more solid connection between the two Census reports, I relied on World War I and World War II draft registration cards for John, Adolph, and Otto, as well as historic address directories.[3] The last two pieces of information I used to confirm that John Stroebele was my great-grandfather was the 1930 Census report showing him living with my grandmother and her 12 young children, and his naturalization papers.[4] The age appearing next to John Stroebele's name was *86,* and the relationship box had, "father-in-law," written inside of it. John's marital status read that he was widowed. A call to Aunt Dorothy resulted in her confirming that it was indeed my great-grandfather, John Joseph Stroebele. I was now determined to know about any siblings he might have had. The John and Adolph appearing next to his name on 1900 Census revealed that they were his siblings.

It was in July 2008 when I was performing internet searches for the last name of Stroebele in New York. I came upon the 2005 obituary for Theodore Arnold Stroebele of Monticello, New York and soon learned from it that he was my relative. Looking for someone to contact in Monticello, my eyes found the name of Lillian Goldberg who was Teddy's companion. Much to my delight, Lillian proved herself to be very approachable, and helpful in directing me to Theodore Beebe, Ted's cousin in Albany. "Theodore," she said, "has all of Ted's photographs," and proceeded to give me his telephone number.

After a short introduction of me, Theodore was as equally approachable and receptive to my genealogical cause. It was during our initial telephone conversation—while sitting in my car at a McDonald's outside Dover Air Force Base in Delaware, that Ted proceeded to tell me that John and Engelbertha Stroebele had worked for Emperor Wilhelm I at the City Palace in Berlin.

I turned my attention to some unfinished business with the children of my grandfather's brothers—John Stroebele Jr. and Adolph Stroebele. I set out first to find Adolph Stroebele's children. I called my Aunt Dorothy Borchers and asked her what she knew of them. She told me she only knew of the youngest son, William, but that he accidentally drowned while sledding at age twelve. When I mentioned to her that I found two other daughters named Emma and Bertha, she replied that she was not aware of any girls and was quite sure that they only had William. This confused me and compelled me to search even harder for them. I remembered hearing Aunt Dorothy say how Adolph cheated Grandma Julia Stroebel out of her deceased husband's third of their incorporated business (it was originally George Schmidt that had done this). Because of this, Adolph and his family from Secaucus had been blackballed from the family since 1928.

Feeling 80 years of being ostracized from our sides of the family was too long, I felt it was time to try to unite the two families and forgive the alleged business actions of Adolph. I believed that these cousins of mine knew nothing of their relatives from Jersey City and Albany, and I was determined to change that. Finding all three children was the first step in this endeavor.

I proceeded to perform an exhaustive search for birth, marriage and death records for Emma, Bertha, and William Stroebele. I was growing more frustrated each day, coming up empty-handed. I started to believe that Adolph and Helene had only one child like Aunt Dorothy said. It became obvious that a trip to the New Jersey State Archives in Trenton, New Jersey was in order.

I never cared much for Trenton, even when I worked at the State Senate in the early 1990's. I pulled up to the archive and stuffed as many quarters into the meter as was allowed. As I walked up the staircase I was flushed with excitement over the prospect of finding what I needed. I was on a mission to confirm or dismiss the existence of Bertha and Emma Stroebele. I carefully viewed film after film and was starting to give up when I caught what looked like the word Stroebele on a marriage record. I quickly Reversed the direction of the film to find the marriage record for Emma Stroebele of Secaucus that contained the name of her father, Adolph.[5] I had finally found proof of Emma's existence, and was excited and motivated to press on. After a silent celebration, I called it a day and got out of Trenton. I felt compelled to move forward and scheduled a visit to Adolph and Helene's former home on 9th Street in Secaucus. It was a hot day in September 2008. I pointed my car north on Garden State Parkway toward Secaucus, a place to which I'd never traveled prior to that day. I quickly located the house as I pulled up on 9th Street. It was a mirror image of its photo on Google. My mind wandered back in time as I glanced between Adolph's house and his neighbor's on the left.

The backyard sloped down away from the house just as it was described in the January 1922 edition of the Hudson Evening Newspaper containing the story of their son William's tragic sledding accident.[6]

Authorities recovered little William's body from the Hackensack River two months later.[7] Adolph and Helene had serious doubts that it was their son.[8] It was not the physical appearance that troubled them but the fact the body was close to six feet tall.[9] Their son was twelve years of age and nowhere close to that height at his time of death.[10] It was explained to the grieving parents that his head had been stuck in the mud and the two months' worth of currents stretched his body to that height.[11] The explanation was reluctantly accepted. It was not entirely Adolph and his wife that had brought me to Secaucus, as it was young William. I needed to see the spot where he died; the Claredon Elementary School whose students and faculty had conducted a funeral precession for him from his school to his home on 9th Street.[12] I wanted to know more about him. At the home next to Adolph's former residence was a man mowing his lawn. When I called to him, he walked over and immediately revealed himself to be very helpful. I told him the story about William and he said to me that his wife's grandmother owned the very home in front of which I was standing. When I asked if his wife knew the previous owners of the home, he called her immediately. She agreed to speak with me about it that night via telephone when she came home from work. I rushed back home so I could speak with her.

Our conversation validated my investigation and was a welcome bit of positive news. Not only did she remember the previous owners, her grandmother was friendly with them. She pulled out her grandmother's old phone book and started sorting through the pages. "The man's name was Scotty," she said. She then asked me what the woman's first name was. "Emma," I said. "Yes," she replied. "Here it is." She told me her name was Emma Engelbrecht and gave me the telephone number with an area code that matched Emma's mother, Helene's.

Cousin Theodore Beebe received a full report of my findings, a regular ritual that started at the inception of our relationship. I wanted him to know what progress was being made. As far as the suspicions of a family secret, Theodore thought for sure that it stemmed from a marriage of one of our earlier relatives to a Jewish woman.[13] The secret that Theodore described originated from the Albany Stroebele family. After all, John Stroebele was leaving subtle hints and telling stories, telling some of them differently each time along the way while living with his son, John Stroebele Jr. in Albany from about 1915-1930.

Chapter 4

THE MESSENGER

Adolph and Otto were business partners. Otto went by Richard as a young boy and called "Dick" by his wife, Julia Anne, after they married. Together they owned a third of Jefferson Trucking and Rigging Company, Inc., on Jefferson Street in Hoboken with Adolph Stroebele and George Schmidt. The building that once housed the business was replaced by a four-story condominium. The business was initially established in September 1922. A mortgage was taken out for the building that housed the trucks and offices.[1] They transported, among other things, very large propellers for ships. The trucks used in 1928 to haul heavy equipment had to be hand-cranked from the front to be started. This was dangerous to the operator. On many occasions the crank would surge forward from the compression of the engine, often resulting in serious injury to the operator. Otto found out how serious on August 8, 1928. He was preparing to start one of his delivery trucks and assumed the regular position. Either from exhaustion or lack of focus, he allowed the crank to violently surge forward as the engine started. Unable to move far enough from the handle, the crank struck him with more than enough force to break the skin. It wasn't known what area of his body had suffered the impact, but he was sent to his doctor, Hugo Gille immediately. His body eventually grew weaker and weaker. Otto Stroebel was diagnosed with endocarditis and died on November 4, 1928, surrounded by his grieving wife and 12 heartbroken children.[2] The wake was conducted in the family's living room at 353 Webster Avenue, a common practice during that time. Frederick R. Stroebel, the eldest son of Otto and Julia bore most of the responsibility after his father's death. He had become the man of the house at age twenty-one.

After her husband's funeral, Julia Anne Stroebel had to provide for 12 children and the expense of a large house they lived in. She didn't have a job, but was a third owner of Jefferson Trucking and Rigging. She turned to her brother-in-law, Adolph, for help. In the months after Otto's death, she and Adolph reached an agreement, the terms of which were never full disclosed. Sometime around 1938 for reasons that are unclear, Julia approached Adolph and requested additional payments beyond what they had agreed. This resulted in a disagreement, and a lawsuit against the company and a ruling by the New Jersey State Supreme Court in favor of Jefferson Trucking and Rigging, citing that Julia waited too long in bringing a claim.[3]

The picture becomes a bit fuzzier at this point, and the exact time of the following incident is not clear. At some point a bigger, imposing man came to Julia's house and told her that she "had better sell her part of the business or else."[4] Out of fear for her children, Julia complied and sold her third of the business to Adolph and George Schmidt. The distrust between Adolph and Julia funneled out and infected the children of both families. They never spoke with one another again. According to my aunt, Adolph's children were no longer welcome in their home. From about 1938 on, Julia Anne and Adolph lived as bitter enemies. With this in mind, I thought it was time to find Adolph's grandchildren and try to bury the hatchet. After my stunning discovery that Adolph's daughter Emma was real during my fact-finding mission in Trenton, and obtaining more and more records including Helene's social security card application, I hit a wall while trying to find out where she was buried. I learned she died in January 1974.[5] But was this my Helene Stroebele?

I now knew that Emma married William Engelbrecht whose father owned the Sunnyside Hotel, a well-known and financially prosperous establishment in Secaucus.[6] I had a Helene Stroebele on the Social Security death index and an Emma Engelbrecht and Bertha Raisch mentioned together on a web page of St. John's Catholic Church in Lakehurst, where Helene had died. These facts could not have been coincidence. I hit another wall, however, when I received notification that there was no death record on file for Helene Stroebele.

If I wanted to obtain the cemetery record, I had to try a little harder to find where Adolph and Helene were buried. I traveled to the Monmouth County Library in Shrewsbury, New Jersey to determine if Emma Engelbrecht's obituary could be found in an archived copy of the Asbury Park Press Newspaper. If there was an obituary, I could figure out which, if any, of her children were still alive, as well as the names of grandchildren and the location of her burial—I found it. The obituary said that Emma had died on May 29, 1991. It also contained the names of her sister Bertha Stroebele Raisch and a niece Caroline Marchuck.[7] This was the Caroline I'd seen on the St. John's website who had dedicated a mass in Emma's honor. I knew this was a vital link in the chain.

After locating Caroline's address and phone number, I telephoned her on the way home from work, hoping she would speak with me. After a few rings, a strong and curious voice answered the telephone. I explained to her the situation, and she immediately confirmed her identity by saying that Stroebele was her grandfather's name. I had the right Caroline. She then began to tell me a story from 50 years ago when she went to the cemetery where John and Engelbertha were buried. I was impressed her amazing recall and how rapid and articulate her voice was for a woman of eighty-five years of age. When I asked her if she knew where in Germany John Stroebele was born, I was not prepared for what she said next. "John Stroebele?" she asked.

"He married that Bertha Krupp from the big ammunition family in Germany. There was a big investigation and they got into trouble."[8] I was now questioning if I had the right Caroline again. I told her that Engelbertha's maiden name was Arnold and that was the name on her death certificate. "No, he married that Bertha Krupp from the ammunition family. They invented the Big Bertha gun." I needed to go online and research this further. When I arrived at home I immediately looked up Krupp. After a few failed spelling attempts, I found out who they were—boy did I find out who they were. I was bewildered and found myself questioning whether or not this could be true. When I got to some of the more shameful parts of the Krupp past, such as their use of slave labor in their factories, it made me sick for the next week I spent thinking about it. It was possible that my relatives had the blood of Jews and other victims on their hands. Not even the Holocaust Museum knows how many people were killed in the Krupp factories.[9]

Upon hindsight reflection of the other Krupp members that faced the threat of disinheritance for not towing the family line: Friedrich, Bertha, Alfried Krupp von Bohlen und Halbach, it became likely that Engelbertha was faced with a similar fate.[10] However, like her brother Friedrich, she was cut from a different cloth and may have delighted in separating from her family and its wealth. Caroline also stated that after departing Villa Hugel, they headed north to what she called, "the city by the sea."[11] She could not recall the actual name of it. With no clues to work from, it may never be known what city she meant. The German state of Mecklenburg is the home of some of Germany's best and most well-known ocean resorts and could possibly had been where John and Engelbertha had gone.

During our conversation, Caroline communicated five revelations about John and Engelbertha that only someone inside our family would have known. The first thing I needed to do was investigate the reality and merits of her story. The five revelations were:

1. My great-grandfather, John Joseph Stroebele married Engelbertha Krupp, from the famous steel and munitions manufacturer in Essen.[12]
2. After departing Villa Hugel for the last time, John and Engelbertha stayed for a short time in, "a city by the sea," somewhere in Germany.
3. My great-grandparents brought $10,000 to the United States that was given to them by the Krupps.[13]
4. My great-grandfather operated a shoemaking business on Palisade Avenue in Jersey City after he immigrated in 1882. [14]
5. There was a famous jeweler from New York that became friendly with my great-grandfather, because they frequently rented a room next to my great-grandfather's business in Jersey City.[15]

I confirmed Caroline's third revelation within a couple of weeks when I received copies of historical address directories for Jersey City from their public library.[16] The directory for 1883-1884 listed a John J. Stroebele a shoemaker who lived and conducted business out of his apartment on 356 Palisade Avenue. The address was half a block from where Caroline said it was. She had my attention. It would not be until three months later on December 22, 2008, that I confirmed revelation number four. I sat down and listed every notable jeweler on paper and visited their websites to see how long ago they were established. I eventually posted an inquiry on a prominent genealogy email list on Rootsweb.com asking if anyone knew of a famous jeweler who lived or did business in Jersey City at that time. I got a reply back from a woman who was in the process of confirming that there was a place called the Joseph Briggs House somewhere in Jersey City. She told me that Joseph Briggs was Tiffany and Company's artist who created designs for them. I had a good hunch that Louis Comfort Tiffany Jr. was the jeweler with whom my great-grandfather became friends. I inquired as to whether or not he had a grandchild.

In hopes that Louis Comfort Tiffany Jr. had a family, I initiated an Internet search. I came across author Michael J. Burlingham who was writing a book about his great-grandfather, Louis Comfort Tiffany Jr. I found his personal website and emailed him asking if his famous Tiffany relative ever stayed in Jersey City on business or even lived in Jersey City. He responded saying he did indeed travel there, while working for various branches of the Tiffany Company in 1893.[17] Having confirmed three of the five of Caroline's revelations, I was inspired and confident in her credibility. It was time to explore the remaining two facts—the two most unbelievable facts of the bunch.

Chapter 5

EMPEROR WILHELM I

The first clue that Engelbertha Krupp was our great-grandmother came from Theodore Beebe. He had no idea she was a Krupp. He suspected only that there was some sort of scandal in the family, but it had no face. He had searched for an answer over many years, but found nothing. I was calling Theodore on a weekly basis to ask him additional questions regarding our family's history. Over the course of these phone calls, he revealed to me that his mother, Josephine Adriance had told him that John and Engelbertha Stroebele had worked for Emperor Wilhelm I in the Berlin City Palace.[1] This floored me. He said that John worked as a bootblack, while Engelbertha worked in the kitchen making omelets. When asked who told his mother the story, he replied that he did not know. It is presumed that it was John Stroebele. It is unlikely that Engelbertha told her because Josephine would only have been five or six years of age when told because Engelbertha died in January 1911 in Union City, New Jersey.[2] It is doubtful that Josephine would have remembered the story. I was not satisfied with this small amount of information, so I wrote to Berlin and asked them if there were any employee records for both of them, but they replied back that they had no records under the name of John Stroebele or Engelbertha Arnold—her maiden name.[3] I replied back, asking if the records were destroyed during the allied bombing of the palace during World War II, but never received a response. I did learn later that the palace in Berlin sustained only minor damage during the war, but that it was demolished by the East German government around 1950.

The location of the palace's kitchen where Engelbertha worked was in the rear of the palace, in a smaller attached building. Photographs on a German website displayed photographs before and after the palace was destroyed. It would be a place I would have very much liked to visit, but thanks to the East German government who turned it into rubble, it was the United States' equivalent of the White House in Washington D.C. The Berlin City Palace was only one of less than a handful of physical structures that bore witness to my great-grandmothers' existence.

I searched for weeks for photographs of the Palace. Early in my research I was not really sure where it was located in Germany. Learning about the history and landscape of Germany was an enormous task for me. The country's borders had changed so many times before World War II. There were hundreds of individual kingdoms and duchies in the years preceding Adolf Hitler's rise to power. Very early in my research I thought that it was the Sigmaringen Castle (Schloss Sigmaringen) that John and Engelbertha had worked in, because it was located in the same town where they lived. However, with a little help from the many friendly genealogists on Rootsweb.com, I was directed to look in Berlin where I found the Berlin City Palace and my understanding of Germany came into focus. It was impressive, but did not appear to provide any protective barriers from would-be attackers. One would think a king would want the exterior of his palace fortified should an enemy force attack it.

The relationship between Wilhelm Friedrich Ludwig von Hohenzollern, better known as Emperor Wilhelm I, and Alfred Krupp could be described as close and unshakable. Upon first meeting Alfred, the Emperor had bestowed upon him the *Roter-Adler-Orden* (Order of the Eagle, Fourth Klass), an award and rank usually presented to General Officers.[4] The Emperor was making his intentions known that would do anything to maintain his close ties to the Krupp dynasty. What was more remarkable was the Emperor's apparent loyalty to young Engelbertha, whom he watched grow from a child to a woman up until she severed her ties to her family in 1874. The loyalty he demonstrated for Engelbertha told much about a man who was largely hated by his followers for his brutality in maintaining order and loyalty.

It is believed that Emperor Wilhelm I provided Engelbertha and John a sojourn after they left their city by the sea as told by Caroline Marchuck, where they most likely traveled to their destination in Mecklenburg from Villa Hugel. The one city by the sea that any Krupp would have visited would have been a magnificent resort and not anything beneath their standards of quality. It is believed that a resort in Mecklenburg was most likely their destination because of its beautiful beaches, but unless some kind of evidence surfaces, it may never truly be known.

Though Emperor Wilhelm I was loyal to Alfred Krupp, that loyalty was not as firm as Alfred was led to believe. It was either this, or the Emperor was plagued with a bad public relations image. Was it possible that he had compassion in his heart after all? The kindness shown to Engelbertha was uncharacteristic of the emperor. It was placing his trust, friendship, and business interests with Alfred in the direct line of fire. Should Alfred find out that Wilhelm aided his pariah daughter, it would certainly mean the end of his friendship with the elder Krupp and all association with the power and wealth of Germany's top industrialist.

Engelbertha would have had to tell the Emperor of her father's banishment and disinheritance from the family and the dynasty. There's no question about this. Did she care? Chances are good she did not. Engelbertha, like Arndt Krupp, wanted nothing to do with the wealth and power that consumed her father and seduced her mother. To Engelbertha, her young spirit was devastated from trying to win the heart of the most important man in the world to her growing up, her father. That was the one thing in the life of a small child more important than wealth, power, and famous associations. She had failed to win the heart of her father, a father who rejected all children, who flew into rages and had extremely strange tendencies. Her heart was mortally wounded and had made an adult decision that she would make her own happiness at the cost of her disinheritance and exile.

Alfred Krupp's banished daughter appeared on the Emperor's doorstep and he chose to reach out to Engelbertha and John Stroebele allowing them refuge in his palace for anywhere from approximately three to six months at a guess, while they planned their next move. If rumors about the two staying at the palace were leaked to Alfred, the Emperor would have no way to deny the allegations. Surely the Emperor was as secretive as Alfred Krupp and did not allow such rumors to escape.

Of the surviving photographs of the Berlin City Palace, none were of the shoemaker's shop. We know John Stroebele was a Master Shoemaker because his occupation was listed on his daughter Walburga Bertha Stroebele's death record dated October 1877 on the passenger manifest of the *Zeeland*, on many Jersey City Directories, and on his death certificate from the State of New Jersey.[5]

The next and final move John and Engelbertha made in Germany was to the City of Sigmaringen, Sigmaringen District, located in Baden-Wurttemberg, which lies approximately 40 miles Southwest of Stuttgart, Germany. Sigmaringen was where John Stroebele's parents had died, and where his only living sister, Emma lived with her husband Eugene Kromer and their three children.[6] Eugene Kromer died in Sigmaringen sometime after Emma died in 1925. It was not known who the living relatives of children Eugene, Emma and Marie Kromer are or where they live today in Germany.

Chapter 6

WHY BERTHA REALLY LEFT

In the spring of 1882, Bertha Krupp reportedly left husband Alfred due to him taking young Friedrich away from her in what she referred to as in a proprietary sense.[1] As Friedrich was getting older, Alfred was demanding and spending an exceeding amount of time with the boy and away from the presence, oversight and influence of his mother, Bertha. For a father like Alfred to want to spend more time with his son, it was unusual, and there had to have been a motive. This was after all, the man who once loudly pronounced that, "all children are vermin,"—referring to Friedrich's baby girl Bertha Krupp after visiting the baby the day she was born.[2] The old saying, "watch what they do, not what they say," applied beautifully here. Alfred did not have it in him to give up any time away from his duties except for heads of state and corporate executives. Friedrich was neither and did not, "qualify," under Alfred's criteria. To believe otherwise is foolish. What you would hear from listening to Alfred was that he wanted to spend more time with Friedrich. There is a distinct difference between his supposed wants and his actions, even after wrestling the boy away from his mother.

How can Alfred have thought that removing Friedrich from school and placing him in a busy work environment was considered spending more time with his son? At this point of his young life, Friedrich was mortally afraid of his father because he was offensive in appearance with his lanky, tall physique and behaved as though he had a severe bipolar disorder. He kept Friedrich paralyzed with fear. What Alfred was doing was grooming Friedrich for the one day when he would ultimately inherit the family business. The two worked side-by-side with Alfred as teacher and Friedrich as the reluctant student. It was reported that Friedrich angrily sulked and was inconsolable after his aforementioned expulsion from the Prussian Army and subsequent return to his father's side.[3] One could imagine the thought running through his tormented mind. It was quite apparent that Friedrich lacked the personal courage and will to stand up to his father without the help of the Prussian Army. Some people are paralyzed with fear by another and forced to remain in a troubling situation. In Friedrich's case this could be no further from the truth.

Friedrich was nearing twenty-seven years of age and wanted to do the normal things men his age do like meet women, get married and have children. Alfred would entertain no such plans for his son and Friedrich was growing increasingly desperate about the whole situation. As Bertha put it, Alfred displayed a proprietary attitude toward his son and Bertha had to stop him.[4] It was reported that she confronted him on a day when he lost a game of dominos to a member of the Prokura (Krupp management). Alfred did not know how to lose gracefully and today was not the day to announce what Bertha had planned. She told him that Friedrich was in love and wanted to get married. Then she braced for a loud and violent response. Instead, Alfred turned his back on his wife and refused to acknowledge the subject.[5] It was strange because it was not a typical response from him. What was different? Why did the news that Friedrich was in love with a woman paralyze Alfred's ability to respond? Perhaps it is better left to professional physiatrists to examine Alfred's unusual behavior toward his son's decision to seek relationships with women. Bertha persisted until Alfred reverted back to his usual methods of dealing with adversity. He turned, filled his lungs with air and screamed back at her, "Nein!" (No!)[6] In a rare and overdue show of defiance, Bertha turned her back on Alfred and marched away with purpose. Not long after the Villa Hugel maids were telling Alfred that Bertha was packing her belongings, he hurried upstairs and confirmed what the help had whispered to him minutes earlier. Alfred went through a mental checklist of threats while he screamed like a raving lunatic, but Bertha did not give him an audience.[7] She had made her decision to leave her husband despite the strong consequences with which such choices came in those days.

Alfred was quoted saying to Bertha as she walked out the main door of Villa Hugel for the last time: "Bertha think about what you are doing."[8] From what we have learned about Alfred, his response seems somewhat timid compared to the past violent outbursts and the opposite of what we expected him to say to Bertha. Of course Alfred was referring to the inheritance that Bertha was throwing away if she dared to show this level of ultimate disobedience. This was a favorite weapon of choice for members of the Krupp family. It was used against Friedrich by Alfred when Friedrich was a very sick boy, by Gustav against his son Alfried to divorce his first wife, and by Arndt Krupp von Bohlen und Halbach by his father Alfried.

Bertha's departure from her marriage to Alfred was all the more puzzling. She had finally rejected him in a defiant manner in the name of her son, yet she departed Villa Hugel for the last time without her son. This story does not add up. Examining it more closely, we would have expected Bertha to have Friedrich in tow, but she clearly does not. Why? Friedrich would have undoubtedly leapfrogged over Bertha to get out the front door first, yet he remained under the control and influence of the Cannon King. Something else was responsible for Bertha leaving her marriage and it wasn't Friedrich.

It is believed that the true reason why Bertha left Alfred first surfaced in 1876 when their daughter Engelbertha gave birth to their first grandchild in Sigmaringen. John Joseph Stroebele Jr. was born on February 16, 1876.[9] It was believed that Engelbertha contacted her mother at Villa Hugel, who then perhaps made the birth announcement to Alfred to guilt him into forgiving his daughter from marrying John Stroebele. In Alfred's mind, no shoemaker would be marrying his daughter or inheriting the Krupp works should Friedrich fail to bear a male heir. It was about 1874 and Friedrich was not married as of yet. Alfred was not taking any chances and very possibly banished John Stroebele from his employment at Villa Hugel, just as he had banished the handsome coachman that attended to wife Bertha prior to her departure from the marriage.[10] Alfred chose to banish his own flesh and blood daughter from the family and disinherit her. His actions give us a peek into his mind. He is unforgiving (and beyond) to all—friends, family and business associates. His actions demonstrate how deep his ability is not to forgive. Friedrich Solling was Alfred's cousin—and sleeping partner at the Krupp works. When Solling saw the mounting debt Alfred was amassing, he urged him (more than once) to consider turning the vast Krupp Empire into a corporation in a bid to help it out of capital starvation. Solling believed he was entitled to an audit of the company—and rightfully so. Alfred then turned his back on his cousin. This resulted in Solling being frozen-out of Krupp unfairly ending his relationship with Alfred. To Alfred, Solling asking for an audit of the company books was most inappropriate and as author William Manchester put it—was like sharing Bertha with him.[11] Alfred had avenged Solling's attempt to be allowed access to Krupp's balance sheet. To Alfred it was an unpardonable sin unforgivable not even at the grave[12] It is important to illustrate Alfred's response to his cousin's request to see the balance sheet of the Krupp works.

We see a relationship between the punishment Alfred dolled-out to Solling and to his daughter Engelbertha. There was no forgiveness for Engelbertha either. It proved Alfred was extremely revengeful—far beyond petty spitefulness. We now have the motive and the means to convict Alfred in family court. Not yet fully committed to ending her marriage and the wealth and status it brought, Bertha opted to continue being the wife of the richest industrialist in Europe at the cost of sacrificing her daughter. No doubt Engelbertha saw in her mother's actions that she was devoted to her husband's wealth, power and status, but not to her children. After suffering through her banishment by her father, Bertha's decision no doubt crushed what little remained of Engelbertha's confidence in, and love for her family. She would seek and happily find refuge in the arms of John Stroebele. No doubt Alfred was very hard on his daughter. He probably flew into a fit of rage. He admonished Engelbertha, threatened her with disinheritance. For Engelbertha, her marriage announcement could have not come at a more stressful time. Alfred was dealing with a substantial financial crisis that enveloped Krupp works that threatened to bankrupt the German empire dubbed the Panic of '73.[13]

Down in Sigmaringen, tragedy struck the Stroebele household in November 1877. Engelbertha had given birth to a baby girl on September 30, 1877, whom they named Walburga Bertha Stroebele, after John's mother and herself. Following birth, Walburga developed complications and died shortly hereafter on November 4, 1877, and was buried in Sigmaringen.[14] It was not known if Engelbertha had told her mother of her daughter's death and no such story or record has been preserved on her reaction. It is believed that Bertha finally chose her daughter over her husband Alfred in 1882. The more believable fact was that Engelbertha announced to Bertha that she, husband John and their three children were leaving Germany forever and going to America. Alfred wants you to believe that Bertha left him over Friedrich, but not so. John Stroebele emigrated through the Port of Antwerp, Belgium sometime during the third week of November 1882 arriving in New York City on December 5, 1882.[15] Passenger manifest lists of the *Zeeland* confirm this.

Naturally, there had to have been months of preparation leading up to John's advance trip ahead of Engelbertha. She probably gave notice to her mother six months prior to husband John's departure. Alfred must have showed no sign of emotion, or remorse for the situation he created with his daughter, giving Bertha the moral courage to finally choose her daughter over her husband in a loud and violent verbal confrontation.[16] There was no record passed on within the Stroebele family of Bertha's response to this. We do know that somehow a very large sum of money found its way to Engelbertha and taken to America.[17] Perhaps Bertha was responsible for this. Without proof we can only assume it was Engelbertha who demanded it as compensation for being the daughter of the richest man in Europe. Bertha appeared to have been the go-between for Friedrich and Alfred, and it could very well be presumed she was for Engelbertha mainly due to the children's fear of their father. When Friedrich allegedly wanted to get married, Bertha had to approach Alfred with the news and he reacted violently.[18] It could be argued that Engelbertha contacted her mother in 1882 asking for money to make the trip to America. John and Engelbertha were relatively poor and survived off of John's wages as a shoemaker while the family lived in an apartment in Sigmaringen, far from the riches of Essen and Villa Hugel.

Chapter 7

THE INVESTIGATION BEGINS

U pon arriving home after hearing Caroline's story about the Krupp's, I went online so I could find out more information about this Krupp family from Germany. I knew nothing about them and was compelled to find out more. As I began reading about the Krupp family, my jaw opened wider and wider. I could not believe what I was reading. For a moment, I took my eyes off the computer screen for a reality check. "Are these my ancestors?" I thought to myself. "A 400-year-old dynasty?"[1] I was numb with disbelief. I continued reading on and learned that Krupp armed Germany through two world wars. In Albany, New York, John Sedan Stroebele (US Army), Theodore J. Beebe Sr. (Army Air Corps) and his brother, James, (Army) all fought against Germany and Japan during World War II as did my father, Roland Stroebel (Navy), and his five other brothers: Warren, Woodrow, Dave, Harold (Army) and Jackie (Navy) did.[2]

I immediately called my cousin Ted. When he answered I could hardly contain myself. What I told him sounded something like, "Ted, are you sitting down?" He said he was, and I said to him in great excitement: "Ted, I know what the family secret is, and it wasn't a Stroebele marrying someone Jewish." He was silent and patiently waited for me to finish disclosing what

I had discovered. "Ted, our Bertha (that's what my great-grandmother went by) Arnold really isn't Bertha Arnold, she's Bertha Krupp, from the big ammunition family in Essen, Germany. They invented the Big Bertha Howitzer. The Krupp's are our relatives, Ted." All Ted could say was, "Oh my." Ted had managed to collect family genealogy data throughout his life and began constructing a model of what he believed was the background of his relatives. Due to his age, he was not as techno-savvy as many of today's younger adults. He did his research the old-fashioned way, by collecting documents, records and stories as the years went by.

With great excitement I then told Ted the story Caroline had told me regarding the 10,000 Deutschmarks Alfred Krupp gave to his daughter, Engelbertha when she left Germany. I knew I had my work cut out for me. I needed to establish Caroline's credibility in order to move forward in telling this story. If she was right about these things, then she wasn't making up the story about the Krupps. If these claims were false, then her story about the Krupps was something other than the truth, possibly dementia of an eighty-five-year-old woman? Not possible, I thought. I know what dementia is, my father suffers from it and I can recognize the symptoms. Caroline speaks of the present, as well as the past. Her voice was clear, articulate, and she recalled information quickly not to mention she has a youthful appearance for someone in her mid-eighties. More importantly, she does not repeat her previous thought over and over as if she never spoke them.

My thirteen years of experience writing histories for the Air Force Reserve Command kicked in and the first thing I did was begin to investigate her claims to verify if they were credible. As for revelation one, I searched a well-known and popular genealogy web site operated by the Church of Ladder-day Saints called familysearch.org. It did not show the birth, or death of my Engelbertha. I then spent a good amount of time examining microfilmed records of baptism, deaths, and marriages at the Ladder-day Saints Family History Center in Eatontown, New Jersey. I then set up Google alerts for key terms such as Engelbertha, Krupp, Stroebele Krupp and similar terms that eventually grew to over 30 alerts that did the searching for me. I then searched the ThyssenKrupp website and found family history, but my Engelbertha was not included. In addition, I scoured the Internet for any information about the Krupp's I could find, including German websites using the text translator on Google to translate the text to English. I also conducted fruitful searches on Google Books for traces of my relatives. Lastly I contacted various archives in Germany hoping for clues to my family's past in Germany.

On revelation two, I tried to establish a money trail from Sigmaringen, to Jersey City. What I initially discovered was that a significant amount of money was spent on emigration costs alone and far beyond the means of a shoemaker. When John Stroebele emigrated from Sigmaringen in 1882, he traveled the least expensive way via steerage on the German passenger ship SS *Zeeland*. In locating him, I discovered that his name was incorrectly entered on the *Zeeland's* December 5, 1882, passenger manifest as Stroebke.[3] Since the K, key is adjacent to the *L* key it could be easily assumed that the typist intended to press the L key spelling a closer variation, "Strobele." However, the passenger list for the *Westphalia* in 1883 shows that Engelbertha Stroebele and her three children traveled in a second-class cabin, which essentially had the luxury of a first class cabin without the saloon and smoke room.[4] The cost in 1882 to travel from Hamburg to New York was from $60 to $100.[5] Measured in today's dollars that would equate to $2,000 for Engelbertha and $1,000 for each of her children for a total of about $5,000.[6] That is an unusual and significant amount of money for a shoemaker's wife to have in 1883.

Other items of interest were the three bags she traveled with. How does a mother with a seven-year-old, a four-year-old and an eleven-month-old infant travel with three bags? After all, there is no mention or evidence that any of Engelbertha relatives accompanied her to America. Perhaps she paid a member of the ship's crew to carry her bags onboard, driving up the total cost of her journey to America. Further, the distance from Sigmaringen to Hamburg was 489 miles. The only two general means of transportation to Hamburg in the Sigmaringen area in 1883 was by train, or by donkey.

John arrived in Jersey City more than three months ahead of Engelbertha on December 5, 1882, to naturally scout out both a store location for his shoemaking business, and a home to live in. The Stroebele family eventually called 356 Palisade Avenue their first home (and location of their first business) in America.[7] One cannot help but question how a poor shoemaker who just spent approximately $5,000 in 1883 dollars to emigrate his family from Germany, immediately opens a business upon his arrival to America instead of working for an employer.

John departed from Antwerp, Belgium. I thought about this and asked myself why Antwerp and not Hamburg like Engelbertha? I knew from the Albany Stroebele family telling me that our Stroebele family in Germany was believed to have originated in France.[8] Early in my research I constructed a model based on this information for John's immigration from Germany. I theorized that John Stroebele may have visited family first in Essen, then traveled to Sedan, France to say his goodbyes before emigrating from Antwerp onboard the *Zeeland*, the ship that took him to America. It would later be a model that was completely false.

While measuring the distances from Sigmaringen to Antwerp, Hamburg, Bremen, and La Havre, France, I noticed that Antwerp was the shortest of all the distances from Sigmaringen with 412 miles. La Havre was the furthest at 579 miles, Hamburg at 489, Bremen at 465, and Antwerp at 412 miles. It appeared that John was thinking more about the shortest distance with the lowest cost. Why then did Engelbertha elect to emigrate from the Port of Hamburg further away than Antwerp? Maybe she needed to take the next available ship out of Germany because the rent on their Sigmaringen apartment had ended on the first of March (she arrived in the America on March 27, 1883) and with the trip taking just about 15 days, she could have stayed at a hotel in Hamburg until the *Westphalia* was ready to set sail. Another theory was that she made one last stop in Essen near Hamburg to say goodbye to her mother, Bertha Krupp. A third possibility was this is when Engelbertha asked for, and received the large sum of money to emigrate from Germany.

It was unlikely that she received any money at this time because she would probably have emigrated only if given enough money to survive in America for a few years. How else could she anticipate how much money the family would need to survive in America without a solid infusion of cash to tie them over while John secured work and a home? The most believable reason for stopping in Essen would be to say her last goodbyes to her mother, and possibly her brother, Friedrich.

A careful, exact, and comparative search of Stroebele surnames on various historical address directories in Hudson County from 1866-1900 revealed that John Stroebele had a brother, Otto C. Stroebele who emigrated from Germany.[9] Otto, like John, was born in the town of Veringendorf, in the German State of Baden-Wurttemberg. Otto C. Stroebele was a tailor by trade in Jersey City and seemed to frequently move to the same street as his younger brother John. I utilized Google Books a great deal to augment my research. I found this feature very useful and better than using the web search engine feature alone.

I learned that the Krupp family was Protestant, and I thought it played a strong role in why John was scorned by Alfred (the other John being from a poor family). John Stroebele was Catholic and the Krupp family was Protestant. Now I was getting somewhere. Soon I found news articles on the Krupp family going back to the late 1800's in *Time Magazine* that educated me on the family. Not until I discovered the late William R. Manchester's book, *The Arms of Krupp,* did I fully understand who the Krupp's were.

For me, it was the intimate diary for which I had been searching. *The Arms of Krupp* described in detail every character trait that comprised Alfred Krupp, his wife Bertha and son Friedrich. I came away with a greater understanding of how Engelbertha grew up and the factors that fueled her decisions. I began to conjure an image of an independent, mature, and courageous young woman.

To better understand where and when John and Engelbertha worked for Emperor Wilhelm I, I needed to learn more about Prussia from about 1865-1883 and where the Emperor called home. I was aided by members of the Prussia-Roots email list on Rootsweb.com to help educate me. After learning that the capital of Prussia was Berlin, It posed new questions for me. Did John and Engelbertha live in the Berlin City Palace, or did they live in Berlin itself? I was able to locate a German website in Berlin for the Senate Department for Urban Development, dedicated to the history of the

Berlin City Palace. It contained old photographs of the Palace long before the East German government razed it in 1950. One photograph shows the kitchen in the rear of the large structure.[10] This, I thought, was an actual tangible structure that provided refuge for my great-grandparents between Villa Hugel and Sigmaringen.

In addition, I discovered that one could obtain old records by emailing the town's city hall. When I learned that John Stroebele's father of the same name worked as a teacher in Mengen, I located the town's website and emailed my request. I was very surprised when I received an email back saying that they had a John Stroebele in the 1870's and also a Joseph Stroebele who was the town Burgermeister (Mayor).[11] Unfortunately there was no solid evidence at this time connecting this Stroebele with our family. German archives are difficult to locate and navigate through. Germany's recordkeeping is much more decentralized than in the United States. For example, military records in the US are housed at the national archives. In Germany, they are all separated and scattered in small towns and big cities. When I contacted the Sigmaringen City Archives, I was able to obtain certified copies of birth records for John, Adolph, and Otto Stroebele. I continued to ask them what other records they housed and where might I find them. I found my way to the Freiburg Archives in Freiburg, Baden-Wurttemberg, who provided me with the birth record for John Stroebele and his father.[12] I had finally learned where he was born and it was a Catholic church called St. Michael's Church located in Veringendorf.[13] Saint Michael's was a small church and it is astonishing that it is still standing nearly two hundred years after the birth of my great-great-grandfather in 1815.

Before I discovered that John and Engelbertha had been married at Saint John's Church in Sigmaringen in 1875, I had believed they may have been married in a church in northern Germany after they departed Villa Hugel. Caroline did say they left Villa Hugel and traveled to a German city by the sea for a while before ultimately going to Sigmaringen. I located almost every Catholic Church near Bremerhaven and Wilhelmshaven, in the state of Bremen and wrote letters asking them if they had marriage records for John and Engelbertha. Many did not answer, but a few did. This assured me that I would get my answer. After discovering these areas were not resort-type areas, I abandoned my search in them.

Wherever John and Engelbertha stayed after leaving Villa Hugel, they most likely utilized Germany's growing railways to travel to Berlin, south of them where they stayed for an undocumented amount of time while Emperor Wilhelm I put them up and provided them work while they contemplated their next move. It turned out that their next move was to join John's sister and her family approximately 450 miles to the south in the City of Sigmaringen, located in Sigmaringen District.

The exact date of John and Engelbertha's arrival in Sigmaringen cannot be determined with pinpoint accuracy. What is known is that John Stroebele Sr. did work at the Krupp Estate after he fought as a Prussian Army Officer in the Franco-Prussian War.[14] The war ended in May 1871. It was also known and documented that the couple was married in St. John's Catholic Church in Sigmaringen on August 31, 1875. That means that John must have arrived for work at Villa Hugel approximately 2-4 months after the war, given the duration of demobilization and discharge from active duty. He also could have worked different jobs before deciding on work at Villa Hugel.

A third theory considered was that since a John Stroebele was found in an historic address directory living in Essen in 1864, he could have entered military service from Essen, and could have possibly served for a brief period of time with Friedrich Krupp in the 3rd Baden Dragoons.[15] It is possible that Friedrich invited him to Villa Hugel to work for his father Alfred after the war. However, John Stroebele's name was found on a baptismal record for his nephew Eugene John Kromer on June 2, 1870. On it his residence read, Rosna (now Mengen) some 375 miles from Essen. As for Friedrich, he never made it past his initial military physical and never put on a uniform.

When I visited the Hudson County, New Jersey Clerk's Office in the fall of 2008, I was not disappointed to learn that John Stroebele had not registered any business names, nor did I find any deeds, or mortgages in the Stroebele family name. I expected that. John's brother, Otto who also lived in Jersey City, had the financial burden of supporting a wife and 13 children all on a tailor's salary. One relative remembers hearing stories of how poor they were as children of Otto and Sophia Stroebele. Their other brother Adolph did not maintain a relationship with either brother and practically disappeared after 1890. All of this ruled-out any financial help from relatives living in the area and allowed the focus to remain on the money given by Alfred Krupp.

Caroline stated that John Stroebele worked at the Krupp family estate in Essen where he met young Engelbertha Krupp. It was also speculated—but never corroborated that John Stroebele may have entered the Army in 1861 because on the *Zeeland* passenger list what seems to looks like the words Armee/.61 can be ever so slightly made out using a magnifying glass. It could be wrong, and probably is. John Stroebele is also seen in a photo dated 1925 displaying three military medals on his suit.[16] In addition, his grandson, John Sedan Stroebele was said by his family to have been given his middle name to honor where the Stroebele family origins began in Sedan, France.[17] John probably did not know it at the time that his son John Stroebele Jr. would name his son John Sedan Stroebele. How did he feel when his grandson bore the middle name Sedan? John Stroebele probably felt uncomfortable now that he had a living reminder of his lie. Unfortunately, there exist today more books written about the Krupp business operations than about the personal lives of the family themselves. Open most any book on the Krupp family and you will read about steel, cannons—and the balance sheet. They all have conveniently left out much, if not all mention of the children, especially their daughter Engelbertha. This is both puzzling and unfortunate.

Only a handful of family photographs of Alfred and his family have been made available for public view. This may, of course, could have been a result of Alfred purging the family photo albums containing his daughter's photographs. Heavy bombardment of Essen by allied forces in 1943 forced Krupp officials to move the archive of die Firma (the firm) to Burg Botzlar Castle in the city of Selm located in the German state of North Rhine-Westphalia.[18] Not so lucky for them the allies discovered the hidden Krupp archives and seized them for examination, not releasing them for another nine years. Could some of the photos been destroyed by individual soldiers seeking personal revenge for the aide Krupp gave to Hitler's war machine during World War II? There were no reports of such behavior by allied troops when they came upon the cache of archives when the US Ninth Army captured Essen. Luckily for Alfried Krupp the archive of records, documents, and photographs survived intact.

I utilized many of the archives within Germany to solicit records. Those archives included the City and National Archives in Sigmaringen, the Freiburg Archives, as well as the Alfried Krupp von Bohlen und Halbach Foundation-Historical Archives in Essen. While the Krupp Archives did respond to the first few of my inquiries, they abruptly stopped providing information, and instead began referring me to previously published books by various authors.[19] They did not respond to my inquiry asking where Friedrich Krupp was baptized, nor did they fully answer my question as to what was Arnold Krupp's date of birth until months later. I relied on, and was eagerly supplied with information and church records from the Protestant Church of Essen.

While struggling to determine Engelbertha's true date of birth, I came up with four theories, the first being that Alfred and Bertha were married much sooner than their September 1853 wedding reported by the family archives. The second theory was that Friedrich and Engelbertha were born as twins, but the official publicly released date of birth for Friedrich per the Protestant Church of Essen was February 17, 1854. Engelbertha told the crew of the *Westphalia* upon exiting the ship in New York City in March 1883 that she was thirty-two years old—making her birth year 1851, which would support the theory that Alfred and Bertha were married earlier than 1853. One has to remember that prior to 1865, Germany and the international community did not follow every move the Krupp family made. There was no intense media curiosity about them, so it would have been very easy for Alfred to privately banish his daughter without the masses noticing. The third theory was that Engelbertha was born after her brother Friedrich. Engelbertha looks a bit older and taller than Friedrich in the photograph titled, *Krupp family with friends,* supporting the idea that she was born before Friedrich.[20] Because Engelbertha used the alias surname of Arnold when marrying her husband it was assumed that she used the birth date of someone else. How else could you remember it throughout your entire life? Was the birth date from someone on her husband's side of the family, or from her side?

The name Arnold was discovered on both sides of each family. Arnold Krupp, who lived from 1662-1734, was the second Mayor of the City of Essen.[21] Arnold Krupp was considered an ethical elected official. Could she have admired and emulated her proud relative up to the point of getting herself banished? Unfortunately, the birth record from the Protestant Church of Essen revealed that Arnold Krupp was baptized on February 21, 1660.[22] She apparently did not take Arnold Krupp's day and month of birth and attention is turned to Anton Stroebele and his wife Barbara Biedermann as the next likely source.

This other Arnold was found on the Stroebele side of the family. When Engelbertha died from a stroke in her Union City home, her husband recorded her parents' names on her official death certificate as Joseph Arnold and Barbara Biedermann who were both born in Germany. In a record found within the online genealogy records of the Jesus Christ of Church of Ladderday Saints was a woman named Barbara Biedermann who coincidentally had a husband by the name of Anton Stroebele.[23] More interesting than this was that Anton and Barbara Stroebele lived just about 30 miles from Sigmaringen. Could they have been relatives of John Stroebele? Perhaps they were cousins? Incidentally, the name of Anton's father was Joseph Stroebele. Was this the Mayor of Mengen who may have helped John Stroebele become a Prussian Army Officer? It may very well be that there is some kind of connection here.

Would Engelbertha require an Alias in order to be married? Yes—given the unique situation she placed herself in: she was the daughter of the richest man in Europe, she was Protestant and she was three month's pregnant.[24] How do you explain that to St. John's Church? You don't. Doing the math, her eldest son, John Stroebele Jr. was born on February 13, 1876. She and her husband were married on August 31, 1875. That means that Engelbertha would have hypothetically given birth to a full-term baby boy five months and thirteen days after being married at St. John's Church. Those three reasons would be more than enough to compel her to use an alias last name. At a well-known German-based Wurttemberg Emigration web site you will not find either John or Engelbertha on their list.[25] That is because those appearing on that list were granted permission from the King of Prussia after asking the government's permission. Those who did emigrate from Baden-Wurttemberg and do not appear on the list did not ask for permission to leave Wurttemberg before immigrating to America. Perhaps this would be a fourth reason for Engelbertha to use an alias. The emigration officials would have been suspicious. Key Census, immigration, military, passport, and address directory information about the Stroebele family in New Jersey and New York State was primarily obtained from Ancestry.com. I proceeded to access images of federal documents for my use and retention. I built my family tree here as well as a half dozen other family trees.

The feature built into the web site was one that would scan other Ancestry.com member's trees and report back if there were any matches to the family information in my tree. Usually an Ancestor hint would appear next to the person in the family tree that would flag the person in question. You would be provided with a hyperlink to click on to see what significant documents were found about your relative on someone else's family tree. Things were starting to add up quickly.

Chapter 8

THE ALBANY STROEBELES

I discovered the obituary for Theodore, Teddy Arnold Stroebele while conducting research on the internet in July 2008.[1] I learned from reading it that he was one of two sons of John Stroebele Jr. and lived most of his life in the beautiful rolling hills of Monticello, in upstate New York. Reading further, I learned that cousin Teddy who died in 2005, was a respected member of the Monticello community and served for over thirty years as Superintendent of the Monticello Highway and Roads Department.[2] His service was so distinguished, that after his death the Neighborhood Recreation Center in Monticello was renamed, The Theodore Stroebele Recreation Center in his honor.[3] In addition, a road (Stroebele Drive) was named in Teddy's honor. As it was told, Theodore was a great storyteller and gentleman. I didn't know it then, but Cousin Teddy Stroebele would lead me to the rest of the Stroebele family that departed Hudson County around the year 1915.

I read in Teddy Stroebele's obituary that he had a companion named Lillian Goldberg from between the death of his wife, Elizabeth in 1990 up until his own in 2005. Elizabeth was not Teddy's significant other, just a wonderful and trusted friend in the autumn of his life. I immediately began an internet search for this Lillian Goldberg in hopes of discovering information about the Stroebele family of Albany. I was unsure of how I would be received by her if I called.

During my July 2008 drill weekend with my Reserve unit at Dover Air Force Base in Delaware, I sat in a local pizza shop when I made my first call to Lillian on my cell phone after locating her telephone number on whitepages.com. After leaving two voicemails for her that went unanswered, I began to think she did not want to talk to me. When I called her a third time, she finally picked up the phone. Lillian told me she did not know anything about Teddy's family history in Monticello. She did tell me that I should call a Theodore Beebe and that he knew a lot about the Stroebele family history and that he had all the pictures that Teddy had in his possession before his death.

I thanked Lillian for her help and immediately dialed Theodore Beebe's number. I was not sure how I would be received by Theodore either, or if he would even talk to me. Much to my delight, he was warm and receptive to my questions and gave me additional information about the Albany Stroebele family. He provided me the names and dates of birth of all the children and their wives of John Stroebele Jr. born from oldest to youngest to John and Linda Stroebele were: Josephine Lena in 1903, Linda Barbara in 1904, John Sedan in 1906, Theodore Arnold in 1909, and Florence Viola in 1910.

Josephine Lena was Theodore Beebe's mother. Naturally, the first subject I wanted to talk about was our great-grandfather, John Stroebele Sr. I asked Theodore what he knew about him. He began to tell me that John Stroebele Sr. lived in Albany with his son John Stroebele Jr. Theodore went on to tell me that John Stroebele Sr. was a gentleman who liked to speak German to him and who took a liking to making miniature lead German soldiers that he displayed for sale in the front window of the Stroebele Grill at 55 Ontario Street, until that is, when bricks starting flying through their store front window from unhappy neighborhood residents during World War I.[4] Sure John Stroebele was very proud of his military service as a Prussian Army officer during the Franco-Prussian War, but America was fighting World War I against Germany. Anything German, especially German military toy soldiers were not a welcome site in America.

I asked Theodore if he knew where in Germany John Stroebele was born. He said he had no idea. I knew that John and Engelbertha lived in

Sigmaringen from the immigration records I located online, and I was de-termined to find out where because it could lead me to many more Stroebele relatives in Germany. Theodore said that he had a copy of an old letter giv-en to him by his mother Josephine that was addressed to John Stroebele Sr. and mailed from Sigmaringen dated 1926.[5] Theodore also had a copy of a postcard from Sigmaringen from an individual named Mortiz.[6] After asking him for these, Theodore sent them so I could analyze them for clues. When the letter and postcard arrived, I had them translated from old German to English. The letter and postcard were the only correspondence (and clues) we had from Germany. The letter was written by a Marie Kromer, who was the niece of John Stroebele writing to deliver the grim news that John's sister, Emma Kromer, had died of a stroke on December 22, 1925.[7] Marie did not get around to sending the letter for another two months after her mother's death due to her mourning. In the letter, Marie tells her uncle John that her mother suffered a stroke and died three days later with her burial on Christmas day at Friedhof Sigmaringen (Sigmaringen Cemetery). She goes on to describe her father's anguish as he threw himself upon his wife's coffin while he openly wept. Details of Emma are also disclosed in the letter. She apparently never wanted to be left alone and always needed someone with her at all times. This puzzled me. Emma had visited her brother John from Germany twice and appeared to have traveled alone. Did this fear come after her visits, or did she muster enough courage to travel alone to Jersey City from Germany?

The earliest recorded date for John Stroebele Jr. in Albany was recorded on an application for military pension in March 1915. It was determined by comparing the baptism record of Otto William "Dave" Stroebel Jr. of Jersey City, who was the nephew of John Stroebele Jr. The records showed that a John Stroebele attended the baptism on June 15, 1915, as the sponsor. It was thought that it could have been John Stroebele Sr. since John Stroebele Jr. had already moved with his wife Linda and children to Albany, leaving his father John in Jersey City where it was presumed that he was still operating his saloon on Congress Street, but eventually closed his saloon and moved up to Albany, New York where he lived with his eldest son and family. Since John Sr. was considered too old for this baptism role, that it was brother, John

Stroebele Jr. For a man who had a lot of money, John Stroebele Jr. did not show, or advertise it. The family lived, for the most part, above their bar and grill at 55 Ontario Street.[8] Prior to the grill's present location, it was first established on the opposite corner of Ontario and Second Street above Skipper's Pharmacy and was known as the Bleaker Restaurant.[9] When the owner of another restaurant with the same name protested to John Stroebele Jr. he simply removed the sign outside and the grill and operated under the assumed name of The Stroebele Grill, though no documentation at the Albany County Clerk's Office existed for a business entity with the word Stroebele in it.

John Stroebele Jr. was described by Theodore Beebe as easy-going, reserved type of guy who was not one to have a high-level of energy. He was a thinker. Before moving to Albany from Hoboken, he served in the US Army during the Spanish-American War as a volunteer enlistee. If you ask Charles Stroebele he will tell you stories passed down from his grandfather, John Stroebele Jr. of how he served alongside Teddy Roosevelt. US Army records obtained from the National Archives in Washington, D.C. show that John Stroebele Jr. enlisted in the Army on March 19, 1898, while living with his parents at 273 Hancock Avenue in Jersey City.[10] After completing US Army Recruit Training, John Stroebele Jr. was assigned to Battery F, 7th US Artillery during the Spanish-American War. He was honorably discharged on April 17, 1899, in Winthrop, Massachusetts, thus becoming the first member of the Stroebele family to proudly and honorably serve in any branch of the US military. John Stroebele Jr. was the owner of a car cleaning business operated from the family home on New York Avenue in Jersey City.[11] Soon after that he left and became a clerk in a factory while living in Hoboken with his wife and children.[12] It seemed that cleaning cars was not as profitable as he had thought. Still, it demonstrated his interests in owning a business like his younger brothers, Adolph and Otto did in 1922. The entrepreneur gene was definitely in the family. When he was married with children, he moved to Albany around 1915. He sought and gained employment by the New York Central Railroad as a Coppersmith making ornaments and fixtures for passenger railroad cars.[13] When he moved his family to Monticello, he gave up the railroad for more peaceful surroundings in beautiful Sullivan County.

There, he said on the 1930 Census that he was a farmer while waiting-out prohibition.[14] When prohibition was repealed in 1933, John quickly moved with his wife back to Albany where he reopened the Stroebele Grill on Ontario Street. The 1940 US Census confirms this.

In 1927, John and Linda Stroebele celebrated their 25th wedding anniversary in Albany. If photographs could talk, they would tell you that those in attendance included members of the Stroebele Camadine and Fritschie families. They all came in their best dress. Two photographs taken that day in the backyard of Ontario Street show a thin eighty-two-year-old John Stroebele Sr. in his suit complete with derby (as did his son).[15] Linda Stroebele posed in a photograph with husband John Stroebele Jr. wearing an expensive fur coat and hat. The point I am making is that John said he was a Coppersmith working for the New York Central Railroad. How they were able to afford the formal attire they had was beyond me. More importantly, why did they have expensive suits and fur coats? Chances are very good that you would not see fellow railroad workers who could afford these clothes let alone want to dress this way.

The Stroebele family of Albany were parishioners of St. Patrick's Roman Catholic Church on Central Avenue, although the family rarely went to church.[16] Job-one for John Stroebele Jr. was to tend to all aspects of the family business, even on Sundays. It is believed that most of John and Linda's children completed Holy Communion and confirmation at St. Patrick's with the exception of Josephine, who completed both while still living in Hoboken.

One block west of the Stroebele grill was Swinburne Park where John Stroebele Sr. was said to have gone frequently for relaxation. It was a very large park with a baseball diamond and was surrounded by an iron fence. He would bring his three Prussian Army medals with him to polish them, and if you were lucky, he would tell you a story from his younger days as a Prussian Army Officer. No doubt his only audience were the trees, squirrels and the birds and it was not known who the recipient of his medals were when he died, but it was reported that in the Jersey City home of Julia Stroebel were various Franco-Prussian War artifacts.[17] Where those artifacts are today remains unknown. Julia Stroebel was said to have these items in her home prior to 1950.

When prohibition reared its head in 1920, John Stroebele Jr. like all businesses that served alcohol was ordered to stop the sale of them, or close his doors. Faced with the loss of revenue from this, he rented the lower floor of 55 Ontario Street which housed the Stroebele Grill, packed his family up and moved some 110 miles south to the Township of Thompson, New York, a suburb of Monticello where his wife's parents, Theodore and Christina Fritschie lived on a farm on South Woods Road once owned by a James Fletcher.[18] Why he abandoned his idea of being a food-only establishment requires closer examination. It seemed like a good and sensible idea for a man who had a family to support. Yet, he chose not to continue operating the Grill without alcohol. It can be argued that this is because he had more than enough money to support his family, who by now were married with children of their own, and he wanted to take a vacation away from any form of work. What better place to take a vacation than in the quiet hills of Thompson near his son, Teddy Stroebele.

John Stroebele Jr. maintained his property at 55 Ontario Street in Albany while on hiatus in Monticello. He bought a lot containing a farmhouse at 41 South Woods Drive, next door to his father-in-law, Theodore Fritschie, who was already operating rental bungalows where he would grow fruits and vegetables on his farm and offer them, along with ice to his renters. He was the kind of resourceful businessman that John and Linda admired and emulated through the years. In fact, on the 1930 Census, John Stroebele Jr. stated his occupation was a farmer, a testament to how he emulated Theodore Fritschie in a quest to attain success.[19] John Stroebele Jr. gave up a life that he knew worked on Ontario Street, for one he had no idea at all if he would like, or would be profitable. It doesn't make sense. It was not readily known how long John Stroebele Jr. was a farmer, but it is known that he eventually gave up that occupation and Monticello for the hustle and bustle of city life in Albany when prohibition ended on December 5, 1933.

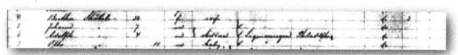

SS *Westphalia* Passenger Manifest showing Engelbertha Stroebele and sons John, Adolph, and Otto. March 27, 1883, (courtesy Ancestry.com).

Map of Sigmaringen, Baden-Wurttemberg, Germany,
(courtesy Wikimedia Commons).

Villa Hugel- Krupp Estate in Essen (courtesy Wikimedia Commons).

Krupp family with friends- Photograph from the book, *Pictures of Krupp: Photography and History in the Industrial Age,* One of the strongest piece of evidence showing Engelbertha Krupp (lower-left) wrongly identified as Clara Bruch, sitting next to mother Bertha Krupp c. 1868/69. Only known photograph to exist showing Engelbertha with parents and brother Friedrich (courtesy Alfried Krupp von Bohlen und Halbach Foundation- Krupp Historical Archive).

First of two photographs of the real Clara Bruch from author
Christopher Fifield's book, *Max Bruch: His Life and Works*
(courtesy Max Bruch Archive, Cologne, Germany).

Clara Bruch-wife of German composer Max Bruch (courtesy
Max Bruch Archive, Cologne, Germany).

Friedrich, Alfred, and Bertha Krupp as they appear in a Photograph on the ThyssenKrupp web site. Is it plausible that this photograph was cut to exclude Engelbertha to the left of Friedrich? c.1869 (courtesy Alfried Krupp von Bohlen und Halbach Foundation- Krupp Historical Archive).

Alfred Krupp c.1855 (courtesy Alfried Krupp von Bohlen und
Halbach Foundation-Krupp Historical Archive).

Krupp Big Bertha Howitzer (courtesy Wikimedia Commons).

Germany's U-boat Program began with SM U-1 designed by Krupp engineers in 1906 (courtesy Wikimedia Commons).

Bertha Krupp, nee Eichhoff, c. 1860's (courtesy Alfried Krupp von
Bohlen und Halbach Foundation-Krupp Historical Archive).

Friedrich Alfred "Fritz" Krupp (1854-1902), brother To Engelbertha Krupp
Stroebele-The Second Cannon King (courtesy Wikimedia Commons).

Bertha Krupp with son Friedrich, c.1857. (courtesy Alfried Krupp von Bohlen und Halbach Foundation-Krupp Historical Archive).

Friedrich Alfred Krupp, 1873. (courtesy Alfried Krupp von Bohlen
und Halbach Foundation-Krupp Historical Archive).

Gustav Krupp von Bohlen und Halbach (courtesy Wikimedia Commons).

Wilhelm I, Emperor of Prussia. Reigned from 1861-1888
(courtesy Wikimedia Commons).

Royal City Palace, Berlin, Germany c. 1900 (courtesy Wikimedia Commons).

Wilhelm II, Emperor of Prussia. Reigned from 1888-
1918 (courtesy Wikimedia Commons).

St. John's Catholic Church, Sigmaringen, Baden-Wurttemberg, Germany where John and Engelbertha Stroebele were married in 1875 (courtesy Sigmaringen.de).

Castle Garden Immigration Center in Lower Manhattan where John and Engelbertha Stroebele arrived by steamship from Germany, c.1961 (courtesy Wikimedia Commons).

HERMANN | **LAGER BEER BREWERY,** | **BURR, SON & CO., Prop's,** 221, 223, 225, 232, 234 W. 18th St., **N.Y.**

| STR | 436 | STR |

Stratford Jennie, sewing, 246 Bay
Stratford Robert J, oakum, 57 Linden av
Stratford William G, clerk, 125 Summit av
Strathman Anna, wid John, 46 Grand, H'n
Stratton John J, pilot, 270 2d
Stratton Thomas, fireman, 7 Jackson av
Stratz George, blacksmith, Cator av n Ocean av, h Terhune av n Bergen av
Straub August, weaver, 74 Thorne
Straub John, shoes, 276 Bloomfield, H'n
Straube Max, engineer, 47 Wash'n, H'n
Straughn Frederick, physician, 197½ Bergen av
Straughd John E, porter, 70 Greene
Straughn William, tel opr, 197½ Bergen av
Straus Bertha, wid Christian, 170 Wash'n, H'n
Strauss Arthur, bookkpr, 330 Garden, H'n
Strauss Charles, clerk, 87 Wash'n, H'n
Strauss Frederick, agent, 330 Garden, H'n
Strauss Paul, bookkpr, 330 Garden, H'n
Stray John, engineer, 756 Jersey av
Straziuso Prospero, shoemkr, Fisk n Mallory av
Strebeck Charles, pencilmkr, 45 Manhattan av
Strebel Frederick, lab, 65 Morris
Streble Henry, driver, 48 York
Streck Frederick, contractor, r 175 Newark av
STRECKFUSS CHARLES F. Bellevue Park, best accommodations for picnics, balls, etc, 40 Ogden av c Franklin
Street Charles G (Detwiller & Street), N Y
Street James, mariner, 168 Brunswick
Street Thomas, foreman, 47 Chestnut av
Street Thomas, watchmkr, 36 High
Street William, polisher, 36 High
Street William jr, engraver, 36 High
Streiber George E, butcher, r 98 Bright
Streinline Augustus, mariner, 115 9th
Streit Charles, baker, 104 6th, H'n
Strenchert Joseph, grocer, 26 Beacon av
Streng Elise, drygds, 134 1st, H'n
STRENG GUSTAV, commissioner for all States and justice of the peace, 84 Wash'n, H'n
Strenge Michael, foreman, ft Wash'n
Stresney Peter, lab, 106 Essex
Stretch Eliskim S, vinegar, 58 Grand, H'n, h Orange, N J
Stretch Phebe, corsetmkr, 342 Monmouth
Stretch William B, driver, 75 1st, H'n
Stretz Andrew, sponger, 136 Clinton, H'n
Stribeg William P, photgr, 45 Monroe, H'n
Stricker Frederick, shoemkr, 374 Palisade av
Strickham Marcus D, 2 Magnolia av
Strickland Henry A, printer, 211 6th
Strickland James, driver, 302 7th
Strickland Thomas, engineer, 25 Waverly
Strickland William H, engineer, 41 Waverly
Stringer Anne, wid George F, 574 Newark av
Stringer Benjamin, printer, 391 Grove
Stringer Edmund, clerk, 391 Grove
Stringer Edward F, clerk, 391 Grove

Stringer Henry B, clerk, 574 Newark av
Stringer William M, machinist, 574 Newark av
Stringham Gertrude, dressmkr, 56 Harrison av
Stringham John W, watchman, 72 Lex av
Stritter George, lab, Prospect n Central av
Strobel Charles, polisher, 185 Zabriskie
Strobel Henry, lab, 11 Clinton, H'n
Strobel Max, porter, 71 Thorne
Stroebele John, shoemkr, 356 Palisade av
Strober Joseph W, clerk, 15 Brinkerhoff
Strober Otto, tailor, 234 South
Stroby Anna C, teacher, 237 Barrow
Stroby Harry, calker, 237 Barrow
Stroby Sarah, wid Peter, 237 Barrow
Strscker John G, saloon, 416 Newark av, h 489 Pavonia av
Stroedel Christian, butcher, 390 2d
Stroh Frederick, toolmkr, 115 Franklin
Strohmeyer Henry W (Strohmeyer & Kiel), 264 3d
Strohmeyer & Kiel (Henry W Strohmeyer and George Kiel), grocers, 381 Grove
Strohsahl Henry F, produce, 163 1st, H'n
Strong Edward, foreman, 129 Pavonia av
Strong Mulford R, conductor, 3 Willow ct
Strother Henry, broker, 58 River, H'n
STROTHER EDWARD H (Schroeder & Strother), 2d c River, H'n
Strohhoefer Killian, cutter, 387 Germania av
Strothmann Henry, grocer, 77 Laidlaw av
Strothoff Henry J, salesman, 280 Bloomfield, H'n
Stroubel Jacob, clerk, 210 3d
Strousher Ferdinand A, gasfitter, 114 Clinton, H'n
Strub Felix, lab, 208 6th
Strube Henry, carp, 161 Monroe, H'n
Strube John, tailor, 132 Beacon av
Strubeg Charlotte, wid August, 104 Garden, H'n
Strubeg William, photgr, 69 Adams, H'n
Strubel Frank, shoemkr, Fulton av n Ocean av
Strubel Henry F, hostler, 13 Harrison, H'n
Struble Albert A, conductor, 290 4th
Struble Isaac J (Struble & Voetter), 99 Wayne
Struble Peter C, driver, 836 Bergent pt plk rd
Struble & Voetter (Isaac J Struble and Julius Voetter), butchers, 6th
Struck Ernst, cigars, 253 Wash'n, h 52 Montg'y
Struckmann Frederick, clerk, 70 7th, H'n
Struele Jacob, plumber, 125 South
Struefren William, carp, 101 Willow, H'n
Strugnell Albert, clerk, 331 Park av, H'n
Strugnell Henry, foreman, 122 Wayne
Strumber Charles, lab, 42 Sussex
Strunck John A, saloon, 128 Newark, h 3 Cottage Row, H'n
Struppmann Charles, harnessmkr, 28 Beacon av
Struthers Mary, wid James, 113 Oak

HANKS' JOINTLESS DENTURE, { **E. F. HANKS,** Dentist, } Grove, cor. York, J. C.

Gopsill's 1883-84 Jersey City Directory (courtesy Ancestry.com).

356 Palisade Avenue, Jersey City. Site of John and Engelbertha Stroebele's first home after emigrating from Germany in 1882 and 1883 (courtesy John Hallanan, President, Jersey City Landmarks Conservancy).

Map showing Jersey City, Monticello, and Albany (courtesy nationalatlas.gov).

Engelbertha Krupp Stroebele. Photograph taken at Sol Young
Studios, New York c.1906 (courtesy Charles M. Stroebele).

Emma Kromer, John Stroebele Sr. and Engelbertha Krupp Stroebele.
Jersey City. November 26, 1906, (courtesy Charles M. Stroebele).

Emma Kromer in Sigmaringen, Baden-Wurttemberg,
Germany, c. 1878. (courtesy Charles M. Stroebele).

Emma Kromer photograph taken at J.H. Smith Photography Studio on Broad Street, Newark, New Jersey c. 1892 (courtesy Charles M. Stroebele).

Emma Kromer photograph taken at Sol Young Studios in New York City c.1906 (courtesy Charles M. Stroebele).

Emma Kromer photograph taken at F. Kugler Hof-photograph, Sigmaringen, Baden-Wurttemberg, Germany, c.1914 (courtesy Charles M. Stroebele).

Emma and Marie Kromer. Photograph taken in Sig-maringen, Baden-Wurttemberg, Germany, c.1885 (courtesy Charles M. Stroebele).

John Joseph Stroebele Jr. (top-left), John Joseph Stroebele Sr. (bottom-left), c. 1926. Albany, New York (courtesy Theodore J. Beebe Sr.).

John Stroebele Jr. and wife Linda Barbara Fritschie Stroebele
c.1927 (courtesy Theodore J. Beebe Sr.).

Bertha Krupp Stroebele New Jersey Certificate and Record of Death.
January 28, 1911, (courtesy New Jersey State Archive).

Caroline Marchuck. Great-granddaughter to John
Stroebele Sr. (courtesy David G. Stroebel).

Laura Beebe, Theodore J. Beebe Sr. and daughter
Faith (courtesy Theodore J. Beebe Sr.).

Wedding day, Gloria Stroebel and Peter O.E. Bekker
Sr. 1949 (courtesy Peter O.E. Bekker Jr.).

Chapter 9

THE JERSEY CITY
MONEY TRAIL

In 1883 when John and Engelbertha Stroebele settled in Jersey City, they began leaving a trail of suspicious spending. For a family whose patriarch, for the most part, was in a low-paying profession, there was a very large sum of money to pay for things, the sources of which could hardly be accounted for. John made and repaired shoes for a living and competition was tough in 1883 Jersey City. Yet John Stroebele immediately set up a shoe and boot making and repair business complete with materials, tools, and supplies inside his apartment on Palisade Avenue and conducted business on the sidewalk despite the odds against him.[1] This is peculiar considering the cost of their voyage, their home and John's meager salary. One would think that the financial strain placed upon them from the cost of the four second-class tickets for Engelbertha and her three children would have been enough to cripple them financially. In 1883 the cost for each second-class ticket was approximately $60-$90 each in the year 1883.[2] The cost for a child was roughly half the cost for an adult ticket, and the difference between a first-class ticket and second-class ticket was merely the access to the saloon onboard the ship for an additional fee. It could be argued that since Engelbertha had children and a very large sum of diamonds and or gold coins in her possession, she did not spend the additional money for the first class ticket. She had to guard both her children and the fortune she was carrying with her life.

Since John Stroebele had two older brothers that were already living in Jersey City prior to his emigration, it was logical to believe that brother Adolph was the one he stayed with his first night in America, although just scant references of his existence could be found on Census and address directories of that time. Brother Otto already had started a family (eventually 15 children after wife Sophie's pleads of, "no more,") but Adolph was not even married yet, so it was believed this is why he may have stayed with Adolph and not Otto. Although the location of Adolph's residence could not be determined on local address directories, he was located on records as emigrating from the same area, month, and year in Germany as brother Otto.[3] The most logical theory as to why Adolph did not appear in local historic address books in Hudson County is because he most likely shared a residence with another person and was not the owner.

It was believed that John paid approximately $40 for his own passage in steering when he immigrated to America aboard the *Zeeland* along with a total of approximately $80. it cost Engelbertha for her second-class ticket and approximately $40. for each of the three children's tickets for a total of approximately $240.[4] Fares varied from different ship lines just as they do today. According to the website measuringworth.com, in 2008, $240. from 1883 is worth anywhere between $4,940 and $5,320 using the Consumer Price Index; GDP deflator; unskilled wage; nominal GDP per capita; or relative share of GDP indexes. What does all this mean? It means it was very unusual for a poor shoemaker to have between $4,940. and $5,320. available to immigrate in 1883 then proceed to display such an unprecedented trail of spending in the years after they settled in Jersey City and onward in Albany up until the 1950s—unless you received a small fortune from Alfred Krupp in Germany. The amount of money in question is no less than $281,000,00. After enduring the financial sting of funding such an expensive emigration, you would expect John and Engelbertha to be financially drained.

German and Irish immigrants were viewed in a dimmer light than any other nationalities and thus were charged more for basic life necessities, like rent. The average rent a German or Irish family was forced to pay to live in either the upper or lower floor of a house in 1903 (the earliest historical record found) was roughly $9 per month.[5] When you multiplied that figure by 12 months in one year we saw that John paid approximately $108 per year in rent for his residence each year. That's like paying $2,725 per month today.[6] When factoring in other necessities such as food, clothing, and utilities, more income is required to meet these necessary family demands. In discussing the amount paid by John Stroebele for the rent on his store, the earliest records available for Jersey City were the classified ads in the *Jersey Journal* Newspaper. A classified advertisement appeared in that newspaper on January 2, 1883, with a given monthly rent of $12 per month. That figure plus the rent on his apartment ($9) totaled approximately $21 per month in 1883 dollars, or $252 annually. In today's dollar it would be cost approximately $465 a month for rent on both his home and store.[7] As a reminder, it was not known exactly how much John Stroebele paid in rent for his apartment and store. The figures above were based on a 1913 study on Jersey City housing and one classified ad that appeared in the *Jersey Journal* Newspaper in January 1883. John Stroebele and family could have lived in a more expensive apartment and store. Without actual records we may never know what they paid.

A search for deeds at the Hudson County Registrar's Office in Jersey City failed to produce any evidence that John or Engelbertha Stroebele ever owned a home or real estate in Hudson County, nor was there any evidence that either of them owned the buildings in which their stores operated, suggesting that they relied on paying the rent on their home and store with cash. This, of course was expected since the couple had more than enough money to start and maintain both a residence and store without the need of a mortgage of any kind. Why then, did they not purchase a home or store? It can be argued that Engelbertha wanted to fly under the radar for fear that any documentation would lead people back to Germany and her past.

Any genealogist will tell you that at the top of the list of the main reasons why immigrants move from house to house is because when the owner of the house discovered his tenants were making more money, they raised their rent. That would explain why John and Engelbertha moved their residence and store to 13 different addresses from 1883 when Engelbertha arrived with the couple's three children, until John's departure from Jersey City for Albany, New York around 1915. That averages out to be a move every two and a half years.

When Engelbertha and John brought the bulk of their wealth from Germany, it was most likely too abundant and too valuable to hide in their home, or store on Palisade Avenue. This led to the next logical assumption that it was kept in not just one bank, but many banks as to minimize suspicion which would lead to questions and unwanted attention from those who would make it their business to know the Stroebele's business. I discovered that the nearest bank to the Stroebele home was the Trust Company of New Jersey. This bank's assets were ultimately sold to Capital One Bank, who by law, did not have to save any customer records older than six years. In Germany, banks were mandated to save records going back only 10 years so there was no chance of retrieving John Stroebele's bank records in Sigmaringen.[8]

If the bulk of the wealth were brought over in diamonds and gold, then John would have had a need to have a variety of jewelry stores both in Sigmaringen and Jersey City in which to purchase and exchange the gems. He certainly would not want to heighten suspicion as to the diamonds' source, forcing himself to tell authorities that the money to buy the gems came from the Cannon King himself, Alfred Krupp. He would be then forced to give up Engelbertha's past and inviting unwanted attention resulting in embarrassment. Explaining how she was no longer considered a member of her biological family, the richest family in all of Europe, would be too much for her and the inconspicuous life she desperately wanted for herself and her family. In terms of what form the Stroebeles brought their fortune to America was not exactly known.

For 14 years in Jersey City, John Stroebele Sr. thrived as being known as a Master Shoemaker who owned his own establishment. His customer base began to dwindle when new boots and shoes became less expensive to produce and to purchase. People were buying shoes from larger companies who began to squeeze out the small mom-and-pop shoemaker shops. One would believe that when a business goes under, it is because of a lack of cash flow—not the case with John Stroebele.

When John's business capital decreased, it mysteriously had the opposite effect. He simply closed his shoemaking business and established a different one, immediately opening a saloon at 197 New York Avenue and mysteriously had the required cash on hand to pay for his inventory of beer and liquor—amazing for a man whose previous business failed.[9] Examination of local historic Jersey City address directories from between 1883 and 1900 showed that many businesses did indeed advertise their presence in these address directories, but not John Stroebele. One could say he was not exactly business-minded. To not advertise was a bad decision and one could assume it ultimately contributed to the fall of the business. The only reason why John was able to open a saloon after his shoemaking business failed was the fact that he had more than enough cash he needed in the bank from Germany to do so thanks to Alfred Krupp.

Growing up in Jersey City, the children of John and Engelbertha Stroebele thrived. Their sons did attend at least grammar school in Jersey City since records at the Jersey City Free Public Library confirm this. Near the turn of the century there were not enough schools for all the children. The ones that were able to attend school were usually the girls while the boys started working at a very young age (about 12).[10] John Stroebele Jr. married Linda Barbara Fritschie at the Weehawken home of his cousin, Clara Schoneberg in 1902. Together, they raised five children while living in West Hoboken (now Union City). The middle son, Adolph, celebrated his seventh birthday the day he stepped foot in America on March 27, 1883. Adolph became interested in mechanics, married a girl named Magdalena Lamprecht (who later went by Helene) in 1902 and co-owned a trucking and rigging company with his younger brother, Otto and another man named George P. Schmidt. Adolph lived most of his adult life in Secaucus. The youngest was Otto, my grandfather who went by the name Richard. The business was a successful Stroebele endeavor. It was also the only bona fide registered business by the family.

John and Engelbertha kept their children in the dark regarding their secret wealth and family history while growing up in Jersey City and after starting families of their own. Before being married in 1906, Otto Stroebele worked as a driver for R. Doughty located in the building now occupied by the Hoboken Volunteer Ambulance Corp at 707 Clinton Street.[11] There was evidence found in the Hudson County Registrar's Office by way of a deed that Otto Stroebele and wife Julia owned a home on Sherman Avenue in 1921.[12]

A second deed was discovered showing Otto and Julia's purchase of 353 Webster Avenue in November 1927 (less than one year before Otto's death).[13] On July 31, 1925, Jefferson Trucking and Rigging Co. Inc., purchased 3 lots—each measuring 75 feet by 100 feet in Hoboken containing approximately 67,500 total square feet for the sum of $1 for the exclusive purpose of establishing operations in Hoboken.[14] Up until now it was not suspected that John and Engelbertha Stroebele gave their two sons financial support. It was quite possible now. It was just too much property—two homes and three business-zoned lots totaling over 67,000 square feet—for a man with 12 children to have amassed. It is obvious that my Otto and Adolph wanted to keep the amount they paid for the land to themselves, a practice that was more than tolerated back then.

Chapter 10

THE ALBANY MONEY TRAIL

After Engelbertha's death in 1911 from a stroke, John Stroebele Jr. trans-planted his life as he knew it from Jersey City, to a new life 150 miles away in Albany, New York with his wife and 5 children. The first public document placing him there was the pension application he completed in March 1915 for his US Army service during the Spanish-American War. The last record placing his father John Stroebele Sr. in Jersey City was a baptismal record of his grandson, Otto "Dave" Stroebel, on June 15, 1915.[1] It was sometime after this date that John, Sr. move to Albany to be with his son and his family. It was not recorded, or even known if he wanted to go to Albany. While his sons Adolph and Otto lived in Secaucus and Jersey City, Otto and Julia were busy raising the first five of their 13 children in a small and cramped home on Cambridge Avenue in Jersey City. Adolph and Helene were raising their three children in an even smaller home on Ninth Street in Secaucus. When his eldest son, John Stroebele Jr. extended an invitation (at least we believed he did) for him to come live with them in Albany, he accepted. John Stroebele Jr. and wife Linda had five children by 1910. He apparently thought he had more room to accommodate his father than Adolph did in the small cramped home in Secaucus.

When the Census caught up to John Stroebele Jr. in 1920, he told the Census counter that he was a Coppersmith for the New York Central

Railroad.[2] During that time Coppersmith's earned an average 73 cents per hour.[3] Upon arriving in Albany from Union City in 1915, he and his family first rented the rear portion of a house on Second Street.[4] Then in 1918, he again moved his family to a rented home on Third Street.[5] One could imagine that his salary as a Coppersmith did not go very far trying to support a family of seven, which was about to be a family of eight, with the arrival of his father.

Of the seven occupations John Stroebele Jr. stated on Census and address directories (car cleaner, clerk, driver, machinist, soft drinks, coppersmith and farmer), none could have prepared him for the sudden and prolonged pattern of spending that took place from about 1923 to his death in April 1958. Though no employee records of the New York Central Railroad were found, it was possible that he did work for them for a short time. However, when asked, Theodore Beebe retained the knowledge of his father working for the rail road, however, had no memories of John Stroebele Jr. ever working for them.[6]

While not entirely unusual if not followed by the long and unexplained pattern of spending, it was discovered that John and Linda took an ocean cruise on the SS *Shawnee* to Havana, Cuba, in October 1928.[7] It was a little unusual, however, that they chose Cuba, for John Stroebele Jr. served during the Spanish-American War and felt the need to celebrate this way by sailing to the island.

On March 16, 2009, I visited the Albany County, New York, Clerk's Office, 190 miles from my home in Central New Jersey to research deeds and mortgages of the Albany Stroebele family. I was excited to finally be able to make the trip that had been delayed due to my family and work responsibilities. My sister, Jennifer accommodated my overnight stay at her home in Saratoga Springs, New York, the night prior so that I could get a full day's work in at the clerk's office.

I was confident that I would find a smoking gun, the trail of money that Caroline mentioned. I had to keep reminding myself that this was actually part two of the money trail that began in Jersey City in 1882 by John and Engelbertha. By the end of the day I had found many smoking guns—just what I expected to find. I felt like shouting from the roof of the Clerk's office I was so damn excited. My discovery had revealed that John Stroebel, Jr. and his wife Linda had purchased (collected may be a better word) six homes in a very short period of time at 53, 55, and 59 Ontario Street, in addition to a home at 462 and 523 Third Street and also 543 Second Street. Keep in mind that they kept all their homes and real estate. They did not sell one before buying another.

The first true and significant sign of unexplained spending began on April 2, 1923, when John and Linda purchased their first house at 55 Ontario Street in Albany from its previous owner, Mr. Carl Moog.[8] Unfortunately, the house's price was hidden by both parties. The sale price was listed for a mere one dollar, typical practice during that time when homebuyers and sellers sought and succeeded in not paying taxes on home purchases. A search of the Albany County Registrar's Office failed to find any mortgage for this sale for John or Linda Stroebele. They had purchased this home with cash, but from where? No doubt from John Stroebele Sr. who was now opening up his cash reserve for the first time in Albany, and John Stroebele Jr. was without doubt the recipient of the largest portion of Alfred Krupp's money.

The second home purchase came quickly after the first. Eleven months later on March 17, 1924, John and Linda purchased their second home at 462 Third Street concurrently with the one located at 55 Ontario.[9] But how were they able to afford another home purchase without selling their first home? Surely, the salary of a Coppersmith making seventy-three cents per hour was not cutting it. Using the consumer bundle index on measuringworth.com we see that 73 cents per hour in 1924 is like $20.66 per hour today. Can you purchase two homes today making $20.66 per hour ($39,000 annually) with your wife a stay-at-home mom? Not likely. Just like the first purchase, this one also was almost definitely done so by cash.

Fifteen months later, John and Linda Stroebele purchased their third home and an additional lot of real estate connecting the home at 53 Ontario Street on June 13, 1925.[10] This time the Stroebele's cared less in hiding the purchase price that went for $100, (costing $ 1,014.21 in today's dollars using the GDP Deflator Index) however, we are forced to assume that it was paid in cash since no evidence of a mortgage could be found in the Albany County Registrar's Office.

In one of many examples of unexplained wealth in the family, in 1930 while painting a staircase in his home, John Stroebele Jr. became irate and began to yell at his young nephew, Theodore Beebe, who had just spilled some paint while getting a little too close to where his uncle John was painting. John and Linda got in a shouting match over this, resulting in John's abrupt exit that lasted for about a month. When he was finally tracked down and brought home to Linda, it was discovered that he had taken $3,400 with him during his stay at the Ten Eyck Hotel—the most expensive hotel in Albany at that time.[11] When he was found, he had spent all of the money. That amount in 1928 valued in the year 2008 was worth approximately between $34,900 and $42,700 today. The loss, however, did not impact them and certainly did not slow down their appetite for real estate.

Among the many stories passed down within the Albany Stroebele family was that John and Linda Stroebel moved from Albany to Monticello, NY for two reasons: prohibition had forced the shut-down of their tavern, and Monticello was where Linda's parent's lived.[12] It was logical to assume that they went where family was. It was said that the Stroebele Grill was forced to shut down due to prohibition. The grill served food and alcohol, but it could have easily stayed in business if the grill offered just tavern food. That's not a new concept. No one else was allowed to sell alcohol, so the prudent thing to do was to adapt, not close an establishment that already served good food (or so I was told) and had a strong customer base with the railroad workers.[13] It just didn't make sense. More interesting was the fact that Prohibition began on January 16, 1920, and lasted until December 5, 1933. On January 17, 1920, a Census counter knocked on the family's Second Street door and asked what the occupation of John Stroebele Jr. was. Someone, probably Linda because she did not work, had told the Census counter he was a Coppersmith for the New York Central railroad.[14] This could not be a mistake since John himself stated on his World War I Draft card just two years prior in September, 1918, that he was a Coppersmith.[15] According to records, John Stroebele Jr. was a Coppersmith when prohibition began in January, 1920. How was he forced to close his tavern and move to Monticello when he was a Coppersmith? If prohibition was not the reason why he and wife Linda moved to Monticello, what was? Prohibition was not the reason why he moved. The true reason was that John took a seven-year vacation from work and Albany in Monticello not because of prohibition, but because there was an abundance of cash to support he and wife Linda without him working.

What was left of the money that was originally given to Engelbertha from her father, Alfred Krupp? That money truly existed and found its way from Germany to Jersey City, to Albany to Monticello and back again. John and Linda hadn't purchased the building in which the Stroebele Grill was located on Ontario Street in Albany until June 1927.[16] This evidence further supports the aforementioned claim.

In another story told by Theodore Beebe, when John Stroebele Jr. initially arrived in Monticello from Albany, he did not work for a number of years, yet on the 1930 Census report taken in Monticello, he stated that he was a farmer.[17] Having said that, Theodore Beebe revealed in a telephone conversation with this author that he has memories of John Sedan Stroebele working on the farm, but not his grandfather John Stroebele Jr.[18] Theodore had nothing to show in his family genealogy collections that John ever worked on the farm. It was observed by relatives that there always seemed to be piles of money when it was needed. You never asked about it and no information was ever volunteered regarding its source.[19] It was believed that John was able to sustain a family of seven without working because he had access to a very large source of money that was brought from Germany in 1883. Public documents reveal that John and Linda remained in Monticello from about April 1930 (possibly earlier) to April 1937 (possibly even later). John and Linda purchased a good amount of real estate in Albany and Monticello for a man whose occupations do not lend themselves to such spending.

The first financial transaction recorded on public documents signaling the very first instance of suspicious spending by John and Linda occurred in April 1923 when they bought Lot 161 from Carl Moog.[20] Lot 161 was better known as 55 Ontario Street, the address of the Stroebele Grill. Since the selling price was listed for a mere $1 and, "other things." When one sees a sale price of just $1.00 it usually is a sign that both parties don't want anyone to know what the selling price was—especially the tax man. We may never know the actual purchase price. John Stroebele Sr. was living with son John during this time and was seventy-eight years of age. Is it plausible that John Stroebele Sr. had begun to share the remaining money from Alfred Krupp only with his son, John?

The second purchase came in March 1924 when John and Linda purchased for Lot 252—better known as 462 Third Street for $2,900 and around the block from the Stroebele Grill.[21] This time the purchase price was listed for $2,900. Today that would be like spending $29,936. John and Linda kept spending and collecting homes and in June 1925 bought 53 Ontario Street for only $100.[22]

In January 1928 John and Linda Stroebele paid off a mortgage of Edward V. LeFevre that he owed to Christina Fritschie in the amount of $806.80.[23] In today's dollar, that would be like paying off a mortgage worth $8,281 using the GDP Deflator Index on Measuringworth.com. Just five months later, in June 1928 John and Linda borrowed $1,000 from Christina Fritschie.[24] The reason for borrowing this money is both confusing and unknown. The fourth real estate transaction that took place in Monticello in September 1928 when John and Linda purchased part of what was called subdivision lot 15, great lot No. 13 of the Hardenburgh Patent from Lena and Fred Ehling for just $1.[25] Of course both parties concealed the true purchase price of the transaction like most were permitted by law did back then.

Purchase number five came in April 1932 when Fritschie sold a 175 by 498 square foot piece of property not to both Linda and John, but solely to his daughter that may have indicated a lack of confidence Fritschie may have had in his son-in-law, though no stories came out of the family confirming this.[26] Who knows. The farm was a sprawling 300-acre farm previously known by residents of Monticello as the James Fletcher Farm that was bought by Theodore Fritschie, Linda Stroebele's father. It was not until 11 years later on October 21, 1943, that they purchased their sixth piece of property: one acre in Monticello from Lena and Fred Ehling for $1.[27]

On January 4, 1944, the Stroebele's were mortgagees to Philip and Franziska Lowe as co-owners of Theodore Fritschie's old farm that consisted of 50 acres of Sub Division Great Lot 15, Great Lot 13.[28] The deal also included all land contained on the former James Fletcher Farm totaling 149,400 square feet. They were to pay the Lowes $1500 ($15,069 today) over 10 years. A home purchased, but not found in public records was the apparent purchase of a home on 543 Second Street in Albany. There is a deed showing the sale of it to Charles Stroebele in August 1959 by his mother, Evelyn Stroebele. But for some unknown reason there was no deed of sale for it in the Clerk's Office, or it was missed during the initial search.[29]

When analyzing the possibility that Theodore Fritschie could have given, or willed his daughter Linda Stroebele the money to purchase these properties, it was not likely, said Ted Beebe. He stated that although Theodore Fritschie owned two thousand acres of land in Monticello, he lived until the early 1940's and reportedly left all of his possession to his son, Florentine.[30] These homes were purchased by John Stroebele Jr. and Linda well before the death of Theodore Fritschie. From discussions with Caroline Marchuck and Dorothy Borchers—Adolph and Otto's family had no money given to them nor did they remember any influx of spending that could have been from John Stroebele Sr.

In early photographs of Otto and Julia Stroebel's children the way they appeared dressed in photographs prior to 1941 suggests that they had little money. In fact, stories passed down from my father, Roland Stroebel—Engelbertha's grandson, reveal a harder than normal life due to the death of his father, Otto in 1928 followed by the agonies of the Great Depression just one year later. My father recalled being dispatched along with his other brothers to collect tin cans and scrap metal they would turn in for cash at the junk yards to help feed and clothe his other 11 siblings. Shoes with holes in their soles were patched with the help of cardboard inserted in them so that they could be passed down to whatever child's foot would fit in them. I don't recall hearing the same for Friedrich's grandchildren.

Vacations were commonplace for the Albany Stroebeles. A regular favorite summer spot for them was the allure of Asbury Park in Monmouth County, New Jersey. They traveled the 190 miles down from Albany with their children. A photograph taken around 1922 shows Linda and Josephine Stroebele on the beach at Asbury Park.

Charles Stroebele tells a story of when his mother Linda Stroebele was ill around the year 1950 and required surgery. He went on to say that his grandfather John Stroebele Jr. walked into the hospital with a brown paper bag containing approximately $12,000 and paid Linda's medical bill on the spot. When comparing the worth of $12,000 in 1950 to 2008, one will find that it was worth in excess of $88,896.20.[31] Very impressive for the owner of a neighborhood bar and grill to have a reserve of cash like this after many years of spending beyond his means, or shall he thank Alfred Krupp?

Another one of the more interesting stories told by Charles Stroebele was how John Stroebele Jr. would accommodate one of his most frequent group of customers—railroad workers. John was a former Coppersmith since his days of living on Terrace Avenue in Jersey City. According to Charles, he would journey to the bank about 10 blocks from the Stroebele Grill in Albany with an empty cloth zipper bag from the bank. He would return home with the bag filled with over $10,000 so he could cash the checks of the railroad workers when they came in for a night's drink.[32] Incidentally, when measuring the worth of $10,000 from 1955 to 2008, it turns out to be worth approximately $80,000.[33] I don't ever remember hearing about an owner of a small and modest neighborhood bar and grill these days requiring $80,000 every two weeks to cash railroad workers' paychecks. That's $40,000 per week, and $5,175 per day in today's dollars just to cash checks.[34] I do not believe any family neighborhood bar and grill today in 2009 cashes $46,000 worth of checks per day. I could be wrong.

Only John and Linda Stroebele knew how they hid their wealth so well. Sure, they dressed their children well, especially the girls. One photograph dated about 1922 in Albany shows John and Linda's children Josephine, Linda, and Florence dressed in beautiful dresses on Josephine's wedding day.[35] They looked like the picture of beauty and wealth, like part of the Kennedy family on a photo outing at Hyannis Port. These were Alfred and Bertha Krupp's great-grandchildren and they fit the role perfectly American Style. John Sedan Stroebele, like many other members of the Stroebel family, enjoyed the game of cards after a busy night at the Stroebele Grill. A game of poker relaxed him and soothed his mind. When he lost, and it involved money, he would call young son Charles and tell him, "Charlie, go down the cellar and get me a couple thousand dollars so I can pay this guy."[36] Charles, barely ten years old, complied like a faithful dog and fetched the money for his father. If you're counting, that's in excess of $16,000 depending what index you are using that he asked Charles to fetch for his victor; yet another story about the trail of money from the Krupps.[37]

In another revelation told by Charles Stroebele was when he was a young boy holding down a paper route. The head official at the bank where John Stroebele Jr. had his many accounts deposited in told the boy in a letter that they were closing his account for failing to maintain a minimum balance. John Stroebele Jr. marched down to the bank with grandson in tow showed the official the letter and said, "What's this all about." When the official explained that his bank had a new policy stating all accounts must maintain a $100 minimum balance. Charles' account was far from that mark. John Stroebele Jr. looked the banker squarely in the eye and retorted that he could close all his accounts too. The banker did neither.

By the banker's reaction, one could assume John Stroebele Jr. had not one, but many accounts. After all, Charles Stroebele said his grandfather told the banker he could close, "all his accounts," (plural) too.[38] The banker's reaction makes us stop and think exactly why he did not close all John's accounts. One needs not to be a rocket scientist to come to the conclusion that John must have had a significant amount on deposit in that bank all stemming from the trail of money from Essen to Albany. The Federal Deposit Insurance Corporation (FDIC) at that time insured each account only up to $5,000. That's in excess of $44,000 per account by today's value.

Charles would later reveal that years after the death of his grandfather John Stroebele Jr. in 1958 John Sedan Stroebele would receive notice of maturation of various bank CDs—$2,000 and $5,000 in value taken out by the former.[39] Clearly there was some forethought to his children and grandchildren's financial future and clearly a barometer of the availability of cash on hand.

During the 1980's, John Sedan came to son Charles with approximately $10,000 wanting him to invest it for him in some profitable enterprise.[40] All of these findings support the theory that John Stroebele brought a sizable amount of cash from Germany and what was left was invested in six homes, real estate, large medical expenditures, lavish cruises to Bermuda and Cuba. It also—for a number of years—came in handy when it was thought that John Stroebele Jr. was not working while on hiatus in Monticello. John and Linda were extremely frugal, but quietly spent their small fortune on homes, real estate, and daily necessities (and luxuries) rather than hiding it in cigar boxes in the cellar where it could have been stolen.

Chapter 11

ENGELBERTHA'S ALIAS

It's easy to understand Engelbertha's desire to put her family and her past behind her. For most of her life her father Alfred was a very strange and distant figure that starved her of the love a daughter craves and expects from a father. There was no love, or affection in their father-daughter relationship. This was compounded by the fact that her mother, Bertha, could barely stand her own ground against Alfred. In order for Engelbertha to overcome her past and move on with her life with John Stroebele she had to part with her past and who she was. It was a difficult time for her when she met John Stroebele especially after they left Villa Hugel.

She was not married and when certain situations required her surname, it either became painful, embarrassing or both for her to utter, "Krupp." That is when Engelbertha, with the help of husband John, came up with her alias last name. It would be Arnold. It was thought that she chose this alias after the second Mayor of the City of Essen and thought to have been admired by Engelbertha and that their values paralleled each other's because he was an honest and productive politician who did not use his power to further his own personal interests.[1]

References to Engelbertha appeared on only six official documents in Germany and the United States. In Germany, she appeared on a St. John's Catholic Church marriage record, the Sigmaringen Family register at St.

John's Church, and the *Westphalia* passenger manifest list. In the United States, she appeared on the 1900 and 1910 Census, and lastly on her own State of New Jersey death certificate in 1911.

It is important to know that Engelbertha's occupation was listed as, "keeper of house," on the 1900 and 1910 Census, and probably the 1890 Census also, but that Census was destroyed by a fire in Washington, D.C. That meant that while her husband John was busy at work it was Engelbertha who was home answering the door providing all the information found on the Census forms. On the 1900 Census, she tells the Census taker she was born not in June 1851 as we expect her to say, but instead June 1850 and that she is forty-nine years of age.[2] She got her age correct, but her year of birth wrong. How is this possible? On the 1900 Census, Engelbertha says that she is the mother of three children with three living. Then, on the 1910 Census she tells the next Census taker that she was fifty-eight years of age (census was taken in April 1910) but this Census does not ask what year a person was born. By saying she is fifty-eight years of age in April 1910 she is saying that she was born in 1852.[3] In addition she says she is the mother of not three children, as she stated ten years earlier, but she is now the mother of five children with three living. Her credibility has been diminished considerably and has made it tricky to know what year she was actually born. Engelbertha is also telling us these years she reported as being born were in fact before 1854 when her brother Friedrich was reportedly born making her younger than him.

Finally, when Engelbertha died on January 28, 1911, of a stroke (as her mother, Bertha had and brother Friedrich reportedly had) the date of birth placed on her State of New Jersey Death Certificate by husband John was June 13, 1854.[4] That too, is incorrect if you believe Engelbertha when she told the crewman on the *Westphalia* that she was thirty-two.[5] While he was filling out Engelbertha's death certificate John wrote that her date of birth was, "13 June 1854." On the same certificate he wrote that the age of deceased was fifty-nine years, seven months and no entry in the days line, but if you check that math then her date of birth would be 1852, and not 1854.[6] Keep in mind that John has all three sons close at hand during this ordeal since John Stroebele, Jr. has not yet moved to Albany for another four years. He could have asked the three of them for clarification as to exactly when their mother was born. Engelbertha's death certificate reads that she was fifty-nine years, seven months and zero days old at time of death.

When you add five months to her death age it will give you her birth date according to her age at time of death on her death certificate. That means she would have been 60 on June 28, 1911. Was this accurate?

We saw two common patterns with Engelbertha's date of birth through-out her life. She consistently said her birth day and month was June 13th, but was very inconsistent on her birth year as we saw four different years when she said she was born. We see from information appearing on Census forms that her memory is still sharp. On the 1910 Census when she is supposed to be fifty-nine years of age, she is asked what year husband John had immigrated to the United States. She correctly answered 1882.[7] When asked when she immigrated she correctly stated 1883, so we now know she didn't forget to tell the Census taker about the other two children she left off the last Census in 1900. She deceived the Census counter plain and simple.

John Stroebele's month and year of birth suffered the same fate at the hands of Engelbertha. For the time the couple lived in Jersey City, the 1900 Census was the only Census that asked for the month and year of every oc-cupant of a household. The following year in 1910, the Census did not ask for that information. Again, it can be presumed that Engelbertha provided the information to the Census counter since John was at the family business during the day. She told the counter that her husband's month and year of birth was June 1844. In fact, it was actually February 1845. How is it that a wife, who is approximately fifty years of age in 1900, is so far off target with her husband's month and year of birth? The answer could be because she did not want the Census counter to know the truth. Engelbertha was covering her family's tracks the moment she moved to Sigmaringen. She did manage to get the birth day and month of all her children correctly. This was more than a coincidence.

John Stroebele Sr. maintained that his birth month and year was June 1844 when he was living with his daughter-in-law, Julia Anne Stroebel in April 1930.[8] Keep in mind that Engelbertha has been dead since 1911. This is the same date that we have consistently seen in the past. Apparently John has been the one who has been more consistent with his birth day and month. Could there be some disagreement between them about John using his correct birth day and month? It is possible John didn't feel as though he needed to be as vigilant as Engelbertha had all these years.

We also see on the 1930 Census that John clearly remembers and it appears on the Census that he was age thirty at first marriage. Correct again. When asked which year he immigrated to the United States, he goes into deceit mode and tells the Census taker, "1884," when the records at Castle Garden Immigration Center clearly show it was December 5, 1882. This is where John tries to keep the Census counter from knowing precisely when he entered the United States. Why do this? After all, Engelbertha had been dead for nineteen years. It appears that John was protecting his wife all those years, but now his wife was dead and did not need his help in covering up her past any longer. It looks as though he was still trying to throw people off the trail that lead back to Sigmaringen and Essen. Why? So what if anyone found out? He was now doing it on behalf of his children and grandchildren.

John Stroebele had firmly laid the foundation of the Stroebele lineage in concrete. He had told them the Stroebele family origins began in Sedan, France.[9] He also told them their mother's maiden name was, "Arnold," but failed to tell them specifically what town in Germany she was born just as he told them he did not know where he was born or what his parent's names were. Of course John Stroebele Sr. knew the names of his parents and where he was born because his parent's names appear on his marriage record. It is there in black and white. Case closed.

John Stroebele Jr. wanted to honor and carry on his mother's maiden name of Arnold, so he named one son Theodore Arnold Stroebele. Teddy Arnold Stroebele would have made his mother very proud to know her son was thought of so highly in Monticello. It is likely that John Stroebele Sr. at this point feared the shame he would have to endure. He also probably thought his children would lose all respect for him for lying to them, so he didn't tell them the truth after his wife's death. How would Teddy and John Sedan react to the idea that grandpa had lied? More importantly they would have asked *why*. That surely would have opened Pandora's Box and the family would have pressured him into giving up Engelbertha's true identity as a member of the Krupp dynasty.

Friedrich Krupp was reported to have been born on February 17, 1854, but how can we be absolutely sure? A check of the Protestant Church of Essen produced a marriage record for Alfred and Bertha Krupp saying they were married in 1853 at the Marktkirche (Market Church) In Essen. When asked what Church Friedrich was baptized in, the Protestant Church of Germany sent an abbreviated and cropped photocopy of his baptism record. It was quite possible that with the wide scope of influence and power over the churches in Essen, Alfred Krupp may have had those records forcefully altered.

Just because Alfred and Bertha's marriage was entered in the church books as occurring in 1853 does not necessarily mean this was true. To what lengths could the church go to ensure a change to it could not be detected in the pages of the book? Perhaps they rewrote just one page of the book containing the entry from pressure by Alfred. The church book containing Friedrich's baptism record should be suspected of being fraudulent unless other unbiased and dated sources of evidence from his 1854 birth are proven to be authentic.

Did Alfred Krupp perhaps pay a visit to the Market Church where Engelbertha was baptized and ordered the church to expunge his daughter's name from all its church records? Alfred had the will and the ability to do so. After all, he owned all the bibles and crosses in all the Protestant Churches in Essen stamping, "personal property of Krupp," on them all.[10] His base of power and influence extended from his wealth and power to the highest levels of the Church in Germany.

It was discovered on Engelbertha's death certificate from the State of New Jersey that the names that appeared as her father and mother were Joseph Arnold and Barbara Biedermann.[11] A cross-check was performed on the Ladder-day Saints Church's two web sites and a startling discovery was made. Not only was a Barbara Biedermann found (the only one), but the fact that she was married to an Anton Stroebele made it all the more interesting. This Anton Stroebele and Barbara Biedermann lived in Assmannhardt, Wurttemberg only 30 miles East of where John and Engelbertha were living in their apartment in Sigmaringen.[12] John Stroebele's grandfather was Anton Stroebele. Could this Anton Stroebele husband of Barbara Biedermann, possibly have been John Stroebele's relative?

What is also known that the middle name of John Stroebele Sr. is Joseph, but there are no Joseph Stroebeles (recorded anyhow) in the long line of the Stroebele family in Ostrach, Baden-Wurttemberg, Germany, going back to about 1750. However, a unique find of an Aloysia Stroebele, a doctor who was a pioneer in naturopathic medicine living just 30 miles from Jersey City in Butler, New Jersey, had a father named Joseph Stroebele who was the Mayor of Sigmaringen, and thought to be the father of Aloysia Stroebele[13]

Remember, Master Shoemaker John Stroebele Sr. went from being parentless at age three to commissioned Prussian Army Officer at a snap of a finger. Who had the power to make then twenty-five-year-old John Stroebele a commissioned Prussian Army officer? The answer might very well be the Mayor of Sigmaringen. Exactly what relationship he had with John Stroebele is unknown. This Joseph Stroebele incidentally was the son of Anton Stroebele and Barbara Biedermann from Assmannhardt. It doesn't get any better than this.

Chapter 12

WHO KNEW

The one question I pondered for months was which of the three sons of John and Engelbertha Stroebele knew that their mother was a Krupp. Like a quadratic equation, I went at these logically using clues I learned from my parents growing up. In 1988, at the age of 25, I became curious about our family heritage. I can remember asking my father twice and my mother once where in Germany our family was from. The reply was the same—"Essen." I was satisfied with this answer, but it was not enough to set me on a path to uncover my ancestors the way the death of my Aunt Gloria's did. How I wish now that I had the spark 15-20 years ago when more of my relatives were alive.

I now found myself doubting my parents' knowledge of where our family was originally from, with good reason. Naturally, I thought that my grandfather had told my grandmother, who told my father. Nonetheless, they were wrong. More importantly, who passed this erroneous information to them? It was, of course John Stroebele Sr. But why would he do such a thing? John Sr. was only three years of age when both of his parents died. It was not known who raised John and his three other siblings, but in all likelihood it was probably one, or both of their uncles on their father's side that had similar names-Konrad and Conrad Stroebele. The first born on November 16, 1820, the other on November 16, 1830.[1] Since both dates of birth are similar, it could be a duplicate error. Another possibility is that the four orphaned Stroebele children were raised by their mother's family by the name of Staudinger though there are no records confirming either of these.

When John Stroebel, Sr. said, "Essen," as the place purportedly to be the origin of the Stroebele family, he was partly correct, but it was not where the Stroebele family roots originated. Essen was where John had met Engelbertha Krupp. He was leaving hints throughout his life but never revealing the big one. It almost seemed that he wanted to tell someone the truth someday. After all, he knew how horrible a father Alfred was first-hand from working for him, and from the stories Engelbertha probably told him.

John did not want his children to know anything about their mother's past and probably made him pledge that he would never tell the children she was a Krupp. She might have feared that one of them would be curious enough to learn more about their wealthy grandparents in Essen. Adding to the family's woes was the shocking news of Friedrich Krupp's immoral behavior in 1902 on the Isle of Capri, Italy in which his insatiable sexual appetite for underage boys was all over the front page of Germany's *Vorwarts* newspaper.

The *New York Times* published the story of Friedrich's death the following day on November 23, 1902, which saw delivery in Jersey City where the Stroebele family lived.[2] If Engelbertha wanted to be reunited with Friedrich, the incident on Capri put cold water on the idea. Capri may have been too much for Engelbertha. Nine years later she died from a stroke in her Union City, New Jersey, home.

It is factually true that strokes take victims after a lengthy period of unresolved stress. Friedrich's actions and death could very well explain the contributing factors in her death. It was not recorded in any publication the feelings she had for her brother. One thing is certain, he was Engelbertha's brother and they both equally suffered under their father. They saw one another as equal in how they stood with their parents.

From evidence collected from aunts and uncles, I do not believe that my grandfather, Otto Stroebel knew he was the grandson of Alfred and Bertha Krupp. It is interesting, though, that if John Stroebele Jr. Adolph, and Otto had lived in Germany, would have been the most qualified heirs to the Krupp dynasty and would have set Krupp works in a much different and positive direction in the years proceeding, during, and after World War II than Gustav, and son Alfried Krupp von Bohlen und Halbach did. Engelbertha would have surely abandoned munitions production for that of more peaceful purposes. One could just imagine no alliance with Hitler, no slave labor, and no destroyed lives.

When Alfred Krupp died in 1887 he left everything to son Friedrich.[3] Where was Engelbertha's 50 percent share in the Krupp Empire? Why did Alfred Krupp exclude his own daughter in Europe's wealthiest family? The answers are anger, spitefulness, vengeance, and humiliation. How would Bertha explain to Germany she had a daughter that was banished from the family 13 years prior? More importantly, how she failed to stop her husband from banishing their daughter. Together, Friedrich and Engelbertha could have navigated the company safely past the events that ultimately led Gustav and Alfried Krupp von Bohlen und Halbach from driving the Krupp name into the ground and shattering it into little pieces.

Remember that Alfried Krupp von Bohlen und Halbach was conceived by an arranged marriage for Friedrich Krupp's daughter Bertha who needed a spouse immediately. She was barred my German law from running the day-to-day operations of Krupp works and lacked the formal business education and experience.[4] If Engelbertha was given her family's blessing to marry John Stroebele there would not have been a rushed arranged marriage for Friedrich's daughter because Friedrich would never have been the sole heir. Saying Gustav joined the Nazi Party because he strongly believed in it and its purpose would be an understatement.[5]

When Engelbertha was removed from the Krupp landscape it had a ripple effect on world history. As a result of being removed from the picture, Friedrich's daughter Bertha Krupp became the sole heir of the vast Krupp Empire and richest woman in Germany upon her father's death.[6] She was wed to her future husband, Gustav von Bohlen und Halbach through an arranged marriage by the Emperor in 1904.[7] That marriage produced Alfried Krupp von Bohlen und Halbach, who willingly and eagerly led thousands of innocent souls to their deaths in Krupp factories and continued to feed and nourish Adolf Hitler and his Nazi war machine.

Perhaps the Albany Stroebele family was luckiest of the three families because they had John Stroebele Sr. living with them (and his money) until 1930, dropping hints and clues that would eventually find their way to me decades later. The biggest hint that John Stroebele Sr. dropped while living in Albany was that he and wife Engelbertha had worked in the Berlin City Palace for Emperor Wilhelm I. He worked as a bootblack, one who cleans and shines boots while Engelbertha worked in the kitchen making omelets—for whom it was not learned.[8] No other details were given and that is all that is known of it.

Down in Secaucus, son number two, Adolph Stroebele was completely unaware growing up that his mother was a Krupp. It is believed, however, that he was most likely the only one that John Stroebele Sr. had confided in about his family's secret. John, Sr. moved back from Albany to Jersey City probably in the spring of 1930, just two years after the death of his youngest son, Otto whose life was cut short at age 46. John, Sr. knew he was seriously ill with what would eventually kill him that June—uremia.[9] It is believed that he wanted to die in Jersey City near Engelbertha and to be buried with her. This is when it is believed John Stroebele Sr. told only his son Adolph, and the story of how he met his mother at the Krupp Estate in Essen and how his mother chose happiness with a poor shoemaker over a wealthy family dynasty. It is believed that this is how Caroline Marchuck came to learn the story passed down from her Stroebele family of Secaucus, from her grandfather Adolph. The key was when Caroline stated that there was a big investigation and the Krupps got into trouble. She was most likely referring to the Nuremberg Tribunals. Those trials were held in Nuremberg, Germany from November 21, 1945, to October 1, 1946. Adolph died in July 1955 and most likely saw the story regarding the Nuremberg trials in the media, remembered that his father told him his mother was from that particular Krupp family and told his granddaughter Caroline. So we have John Stroebele telling his son Adolph in 1930 that his mother was banished from the Krupp industrial dynasty. We then have Adolph Stroebele adding that story to the story he saw in the media regarding Alfried Krupp von Bohlen und Halbach being convicted at the Nuremberg Trials.

On the US Army discharge papers of John Stroebele Jr. from his service during the Spanish-American War, there was an entry that John was born in Sigmaringen, Austria.[10] There was no such place in Austria called Sigmaringen. It was surmised that John Stroebele Sr. knew the US Army was a serious organization that demanded honesty and integrity from its recruits and would punish those who did not comply with this way of life so much so that John Stroebele Sr. knew he had to come clean and admit to his son where he was born so that he could tell the Army, but was determined to keep their mother's past well concealed. He told his son a half-truth, at least the correct city, but he still needed to keep his children at arm's length from their past in Germany. Thus, John Stroebele's three children had no knowledge of their mother's connection to the Essen Krupp family prior to 1930.

Chapter 13

SISTER EMMA

E mma Stroebele was the only surviving sister of John Stroebele Sr. Another Emma, born September 11, 1842, in Veringendorf, Baden-Wurttemberg, died when she was just two weeks old. John's surviving sister, Emma was born on September 7, 1846, in Veringendorf, Baden-Wurttemberg.[1] In 1869, she married Eugene Kromer, a court bookbinder born in a local town called Sheer located in Sigmaringen district, just a few miles from Veringenstadt.[2] The couple settled in Sigmaringen and had three children—Eugene John, Emma Anna, and Marie Emma. On her marriage record from Germany, it read that Emma Stroebele was born in Rotenbach, approximately 75 miles northeast of Veringenstadt.[3] When asked who her father was, she stated, "Johann Strobele," on her marriage record and that he was a teacher in Mengen.[4] John Stroebele lived in the same small town as his sister Emma for approximately seven years after each were married. John and Emma also had two brothers, Adolph and Otto, born in 1841 and 1843, who had immigrated to America in 1866.[5]

After John had immigrated to Jersey City, Emma was the last sibling to remain in Germany. After he emigrated in 1882 they remained in contact with one another. We know this because Theodore Beebe had in his possession a copy of an old letter given to him by his mother, Josephine. The letter was originally written by Emma's daughter Marie Kromer and dated 1926 telling her uncle John that her mother, Emma had died from a stroke.[6] That was the only letter passed down through the years. Perhaps there were others that dealt with the Krupp issue, but those letters were probably quickly destroyed quickly. The fact that Marie Kromer was able to get a letter to John Stroebele in Albany, New York where he was living tells us that he kept in frequent touch with his sister back in Sigmaringen, updating her on his whereabouts so the letters could be delivered to the correct address. How interesting it would have been to read those letters and to know what was discussed. How wonderful it would be if John had hid just one of those letters in a secret hiding place in the one of many homes, or stores he occupied in his various north Jersey locales for someone to find today.

In August 2009 Charles Stroebele located more than a dozen old photographs of who he believed were from my side of the Stroebel family from Jersey City. My family was the only family of the three to spell their last name without the letter, "e," at the end. After examining and comparing the photographs it was determined that there were four photographs of John Stroebele's younger sister Emma, one photograph of her husband, Eugene Kromer and their three children, one of their son Eugene John Kromer, and one photograph of Emma Anna and Marie Emma Kromer together.[7] There were distinctive markings from a photography studio in Sigmaringen on the front and back of the photographs.

Emma and Eugene Kromer were the only known relatives of John Stroebele Sr. left in Germany and when the subjects in the photographs are added up they equaled a husband, a wife, a son, and two daughters. The Kromer family was comprised of the same number and gender of family members. The approximate chronology in which Emma Kromer traveled from Sigmaringen, Germany to Jersey City to visit her brother can be determined by examining the four different photographs from Charles Stroebele.

The first photograph taken in Sigmaringen shows her as a youthful young woman around the age of thirty-two.[8] The second photograph shows an older and slightly heavier Emma at forty-six years of age taken at the J.H. Smith Photography Studio on Broad Street in Newark, New Jersey.[9] The third photograph shows an older Emma at approximately sixty years of age taken at the Sol Young Studios.[10] On the back of this photograph there were three studio locations listed for New York City—one for Brooklyn and two for New Jersey. Since the location printed on the front of the photograph read, "Sol Young New York," we can assume this is where this photograph of Emma was taken, although there was a studio location at 157 Newark Avenue in Jersey City.

A forth photograph of Emma shows her posing outside together with John and Engelbertha, probably in Jersey City.[11] We know the photograph was taken in the fall or winter because they are wearing winter coats and hats. There also are no leaves on the trees. We know the approximate date because a date of November 25, 1906, is stamped on the back of it. A fifth and last photograph of Emma was taken back in Sigmaringen, shows her appearing quite older.[12] Emma's birth record states she was born in the year 1846.

If you believe she truly shows her correct age in these photographs, then the first photograph taken in Sigmaringen was done between the years 1878-1879, or when she was between the ages of thirty-two and thirty-three. John and Engelbertha were believed to have been married three years and living in Sigmaringen. The second photograph of Emma was probably taken between the years 1891-1892 when John and Bertha were living on Griffith Street in Jersey City. John and Engelbertha's children would have been fifteen, twelve, and nine years of age, respectively from oldest to youngest and John Stroebele was still operating his shoemaking business. The third photograph shows streaks of gray in Emma's hair and she appears heavier than in her previous photograph. Again, if she is showing her true age then this photograph was taken between 1903 and 1905. During this time John and Engelbertha are living at one Patterson Plank Road and their sons are ages twenty-eight, twenty-five, and twenty-two.[13] Their sons, John and Adolph, were both married in 1902, followed by Otto in 1906.[14]

The last photograph shows an older Emma Kromer living back in Sigmaringen as evident by the photographer's markings on the back of the picture clearly reading, "F. Kugler Kunstmaler und Hofphotograph, Sigmaringen, Hallau, Schaffhausen." The year this photograph was taken, if Emma was indeed sixty-eight years of age would have been approximately 1914. Emma's death record from Germany confirms she died at the age of seventy-nine in 1925.

Her fourth and final photograph was taken approximately 11 years before her seventy-ninth birthday. It can also be assumed that John Stroebele had photographs taken as a keepsake for his sister when she went back to Germany. Those photographs are likely to be in the possession of the relatives of Eugene, Emma, and Marie Kromer somewhere in Germany, or the world for that matter.

Emma's first visit from Germany was made in about 1892 when she was approximately forty-six years of age and during the time when she would have to come through Ellis Island Immigration Center since Castle Garden Immigration center had closed in April 1890. There is a chance that she could have visited Jersey City before the closure of Castle Garden, but estimates place her in Jersey City no earlier than probably 1889. This makes searching for all Kromer names simplified because they can be extracted from one database at Castle Garden Immigration Center. When a search was conducted on castlegarden.org for, "Kr%%mer," with the percent marks being wildcards, no entries were found that would conclusively pinpoint our Emma Kromer. The closest entry was an Emma Kramer, age fifty-one who arrived in America on May 12, 1893, but this Emma was born in 1842 and a resident of Berlin. The true Emma Kromer was born in 1846 and was mostly a lifetime resident of Sigmaringen up until the day she died in 1925.

An even more frustrating search of the Ellis Island website revealed less. Of the three search results conducted under Kromer for all years, only three had the first name Kromer, but none were born before 1893. The closest match to the Kromer in question that was Emilie Kromer, who arrived on Ellis Island in 1909, city of origin unknown, at the age of 61. That made her year of birth 1848. However, her husband, Conrad was with her. Together the couple was headed for Brooklyn. With no other close leads the question must be asked: If there is photographic evidence Emma visited John Stroebele in Jersey City, why then can't she be found on incoming passenger ship manifests? There is one plausible reason—she used an alias, and it wasn't Arnold or any variant of Stroebele. We know that from a check of both Ellis Island and Castle Garden web sites.

After all these years in the United States, John and Engelbertha were still concerned with covering their tracks. It is plausible to believe that Engelbertha did know that Alfred had died in July, 1887. The story of his death ran in the *Jersey Journal* Newspaper in Jersey City on July 15, 1887. It was unlikely that she kept track of her family back in Essen, but in the back of her mind Engelbertha may have thought Alfred was keeping a watchful eye on her. It was that, and the strong desire John and Engelbertha had to keep their children from knowing about their Krupp grandparents in Germany that compelled them to maintain their secret.

Chapter 14

CAT AND MOUSE

I thought about what information St. John's Church in Sigmaringen had in its church records pertaining to the marriage of John Stroebele and Engelbertha Krupp. He was Catholic, she Protestant. We know this because church records for the Stroebele family on the familysearch.org website clearly show the family's Catholic roots going back to the early 1700's in Ostrach, Baden-Wurttemberg. We know the Krupp family was Protestant from the Protestant Church of Essen. Certainly the Catholic Church in Baden-Wurttemberg would not permit them to be married in the Church without signing a document stating their children would be raised Catholic—and they were. How would she explain who she was and who her family in Essen was? To avoid all the unwanted scrutiny and attention it was likely decided that she would use the alias last name of Arnold.

Did St. John's Church know Engelbertha's true identity? To this day we do not know. The church would not say. [1] We do know that Alfred and Bertha Krupp's daughter appeared in Sigmaringen wanting to marry a Catholic shoemaker by the name of John Stroebele. Of course at this point Engelbertha's true last name was never mentioned to the church.

Email correspondence with the Krupp Archives at Villa Hugel began on April 13, 2009, when an inquiry regarding a black and white photograph of Alfred, Bertha, and Friedrich Krupp that appeared on the ThyssenKrupp.

com website. I wrote to Villa Hugel asking what the story was behind the photograph. I asked how such a wealthy and powerful man such as Alfred Krupp allowed such a photograph to be cut on both the left and right sides in such a way that the cut runs through young Friedrich's hand and through Bertha's dress. It certainly appears as though there was a fourth person to Friedrich's left, but they perhaps were cut out. The response from Villa Hugel was that there was no story behind it and that it was cut for technical reasons.[2]

When I wrote back stating technical reasons was itself a story and to please clarify why it was cut. Archive officials at Villa Hugel stated that it was edited so that it would fit on their web site.[3] However, I challenge that idea because there was ample space to the left and to the right where the photograph appears on the web site and seemed very off that anyone would dare alter a family photograph for public viewing when there was more than ample room for the original.

I sent a letter to Villa Hugel asking them directly if Alfred and Bertha Krupp had a child that died at birth, soon after birth or later in life.[4] Their reply was, "No."[5] After all, it was not expected that the hired staff of the Krupp Archives to know all the intimate family secrets of the Krupp family, rather only what Berthold Beitz and ThyssenKrupp wants them to know and convey to the public. I knew from the very beginning that the Villa Hugel staff knew nothing of Engelbertha and those who knew were long dead.

Early in my emails and letters to Villa Hugel and the churches in Germany, care was taken not to let them know I was writing a book on the Krupp dynasty. They may have become uncooperative right from the beginning. This story was too important. I felt that if I came knocking on their door with my credentials announcing that I had uncovered the truth about Alfred and Bertha's daughter they would promptly cut me off from any information I sought, and possibly preventing the various churches in Essen from speaking with me.

Now it seemed that after questioning a photograph and asking plainly if Alfred and Bertha had another child that might have been stillborn, or died sometime after birth, Villa Hugel stopped answering my correspondence because they either believed I was a novice writer bringing up conspiracy theories, or whispers of an outrageous and unfounded story of long ago coming back like a boomerang to the back of the head.

On July 31, 2009, an email was sent to Villa Hugel stating that it was a follow-up email from two prior emails that had gone unanswered by them. I acknowledged that they must have been busy, but hoped they could tell me in which church Friedrich Krupp was baptized, what Church in Essen was Alfred and Bertha Krupp married, in which Army unit was Friedrich was assigned to before he was discharged and lastly what were the copyright limits on using Krupp family photographs in books by authors.[6] They never answered. I gave serious consideration to the idea that it was them who was playing cat and I the mouse. They were waiting for me to be caught out in the open to show my cards and divulge my information first, although they never asked.

Another email sent to Villa Hugel on August 12, 2009, asking where Friedrich was baptized and where Alfred and Bertha were married. A reply came the next day saying that they were referring me to a book written by Wilhelm Berdrow titled: *The Krupps: 150 years of Krupp History 1787-1937.*[7] They did not state that they did, or did not have the information that was requested in the email, they simply brushed the request aside, not taking responsibility for answering it.

When an email was sent to the Kettwig Protestant Church in Essen asking them whether Friedrich was baptized in their church they did not respond even after a second follow-on email was sent to them.[8] Not until I received a physical photocopy of what appeared to be Friedrich's baptism record from The Protestant Church of Essen did I get my first break in determining where his baptism took place. The sender of the hardcopy baptism record I received stated that Friedrich was baptized at the Essen MarktKirche (Market Church).[9] He stated that he had gotten it from the Evangelische Kirchengemeinde Essen-Altstadt (Protestant Church of Essen-Altstadt)[10].

My first meaningful contact with any church in Essen came on August 3, 2009, was with Stefan Koppleman who was the Leiter Presse- und Offentlichkeitsarbeit (Head of Press and Public Relations) for the Protestant Church of Essen.[11] Stephan has worked for the Protestant Church in Germany since 1996 and for the Protestant Church in Essen since 2001.[12] I did not intend to inform him of the nature of my book. I thought it best not to attract controversy since they controlled access to records I needed. He effectively eliminated the roadblock I was experiencing in getting any of the local churches in Essen to respond to my emails or letters. Stefan provided me not only with the name of the church in Essen where Friedrich was baptized, but also the church Alfred and Bertha Krupp were married in. I may add that he is being acknowledged because he was extremely helpful and did all this so quickly, and if you ask any researcher outside Germany who wants information from Germany, it is either an extremely slow process, or you don't get any replies back at all.

It was imperative that I receive this information directly from a primary source and Stefan did that. I could now be assured without question of which church I was seeking. Stefan took the time to write out the hierarchy of the German Church from the smallest church to the Protestant Church of Germany. I now had a clear picture from which to work, and could proceed. [13]

Weighing my options and taking careful steps, I was unsure of the best path to take. On one hand, I could work my way up from the bottom with the Market Church and stop after going through the Protestant Church of Germany. On the other hand I could inform the priests and Bishops of each church simultaneously thus eliminating the long pause that would result at each church while they scramble to determine if my request was credible. They would also be required to defer my request to their superiors at the state and national level in Germany causing a further delay.

After the books manuscript was completed and all loose ends were tied, the decision was made to contact each church separately, working my way up to the Protestant Church of Germany.[14] The Protestant Church of Germany would ultimately have to oversee an internal investigation that would confirm through Market Church internal archives (if they exist) that they were ordered by Alfred Krupp around the year 1874, to destroy his daughter's church records. The Protestant Church of Germany was also requested to retrieve Engelbertha's church records should their archives reveal something and to make them public. Each Church would be instructed to look back into their past utilizing any private written communications to include Bishop's diaries kept by their respective churches. I was days away from completing the writing phase of my book. I wanted everything about my book to be credible. If they had asked me if I was writing a book before I was ready to reveal it, I would have told them yes. I felt safe that I had finally put all the facts down on paper.

The first inquiry to St. John's Church in Sigmaringen regarding Engelbertha's identity was sent in July 2009. They were asked if they had a birth record for an Engelbertha Arnold who was born in 1851.[15] A reply was sent stating that they did find a birth record and that her birth date was June 13, 1851, with her parents being Joseph Arnold and Barbara Biedermann. This suggests the record was fraudulently created to facilitate an alias for Engelbertha and clearing the way for her to be married in St. John's Church in 1875 and provide her with a cover while she resided with husband John and their three children in Sigmaringen.

Emperor Wilhelm I had the power to help John and Engelbertha in getting St. John's Church to alter its marriage book in the same way Alfred did the Market Church in Essen. Since it was believed that John and Engelbertha did not receive any money from Alfred Krupp until around 1882, it would have been hard for them to try bribery because it is believed they had no money. In her 1926 letter to John Stroebele Marie Kromer stating his sister Emma had died of a stroke. Marie Kromer mentions the family received a beautiful wreath from a person or persons of nobility from the words she used in her letter.[16] She refers to the sender of the wreath on the occasion of her mother's death as, "the princely folk," and most likely the family, more specifically Emma Kromer, must have had an alliance with someone in power and that person could quite possibly been Emperor Wilhelm I. Having died in 1888, the Emperor most likely kept a VIP list of close friends that were to continue to receive condolences under the current administration.

In getting St. John's Church to comply with my requests for information, I needed to use the carrot and the stick approach by letting them know there was a secret their church was hiding from back in 1875 and that my

Engelbertha Arnold was really someone with a different last name that came from a wealthy and powerful German family. With help from the Mayor of Sigmaringen, Dr. Daniel Rapp, St. John's emailed a picture of the birth book containing Engelbertha's birth record.[17] The record read that Engelbertha Arnold was born on June 13, 1851, in Sigmaringen. In reality, stating it was not enough and getting a copy of the record will not be enough either. These books were likely altered by higher powers beyond John and Engelbertha in Sigmaringen, and powers beyond the Market Church in the City of Essen. You cannot effectively erase away the existence of a person just altering a birth book. They continue to live and prosper just as Engelbertha Krupp had. A third scenario could have been where John Stroebele knew the Arnold family in Sigmaringen and took their daughter's identity for Engelbertha's sake.

Chapter 15

PHOTOGRAPHS RESURFACE

Solid and unmistakable photographic evidence exists that show Engelbertha Krupp in Germany and in America. A photograph dated c. 1868-69 titled *Krupp Family with Friends* found in the book titled *Pictures of Krupp: photography and history in the industrial age* shows Friedrich Krupp sitting to the right of his mother, Bertha. To the left of Bertha is a young girl between the ages of sixteen and nineteen who unquestionably bears the strongest and unmistakable resemblance to Bertha Krupp seated to her right.[1] Thus far, it is believed to be the only known photograph to have survived of Engelbertha Krupp taken in Germany with her Krupp family. I could be wrong, and I hope I am.

The caption under this photograph read that the young girl's name sitting to Bertha's left was Clara Bruch. This is absolutely false because the photograph of the real Clara Bruch appearing in a book by Christopher Fifield titled *Max Bruch: His Life and Times* is not the same person appearing in the book by German University Professor Klaus Tenfelde.[2] The photographs of these two Clara's are not at all similar in appearance. In addition, Fifield maintains Clara Bruch was not yet married in 1868-69 and her maiden name was Clara Tuczek.[3] Lastly, Clara Tuczek was just a child between the ages of fourteen and fifteen in 1868/69, and Max Bruch was still a Court Music Director in Sondershausen—he would not even have known her.[4]

In another correspondence with Fifield, he goes on to say he believes the Clara Bruch girl sitting next to Bertha Krupp is related to her due to the strong resemblance between the two.[5] Clara Bruch was the wife of famous German music composer Max Bruch and cousin to Bertha Krupp.[6] It was Bertha Krupp's persuasion that resulted in Alfred Krupp providing financial support to the Bruch family in order for Max to continue his musical education and broaden his influence over those who eventually would realize his talents and propel him to notoriety as a musician.[7]

A wide Internet search for a second photograph of Clara Bruch was launched and produced only one, and it appeared in Christopher Fifield's book. This photograph was graciously permitted to appear in Chris Fifield's book and came from a trusted and reliable source: The Max Bruch Archive in Cologne, Germany. There is an inherent trust and belief in them that they know what the wife of Max Bruch looks like, unlike Tenfelde, whose credibility was severely weakened when he knowingly identified Engelbertha Krupp as Clara Bruch when Clara Bruch was neither sixteen years of age nor yet married.

In addition, in the photograph titled *Krupp family with Friends* in Tenfelde's book goes on to describe an unknown person reading as, "and one other person," seriously undermines either Tenfelde's credibility again, or the Krupp Archive's credibility. One can conclude that the caption was not born from Tenfelde's thoughts. If you trust that the Max Bruch Archive knows their photographs well, then you believe the photograph in Christopher Fifield's book really is Clara Bruch. If you believe the Krupp Archive with the knowledge of their photographs then there is only one conclusion: one of these women is not Clara Bruch. The real Clara Bruch can be seen in Fifield's book.

To ensure the photograph in Fifield's book was absolutely Clara Bruch I contacted the Max Bruch Archive in Cologne and asked them for a different one.[8] Upon receipt of the second photograph I was now more than certain than ever that the photograph titled, *Krupp family with Friends* indeed contained a photograph of my great-grandmother, Engelbertha Krupp.

Another inconsistency in the *Krupp family with Friends* photo centers on Friedrich Krupp. His birth record will tell you he was born in 1854.[9] The photograph in question was taken in 1868/69 would then show Friedrich at age fourteen, or fifteen. However, the photograph appearing on the ThyssenKrupp.com website of Alfred, Bertha and a much younger-looking Friedrich, was said to have been taken c. 1869.[10] Again, we see an issue of credibility on the Krupp side as to the accuracy of the date of this photo by the Krupp Archive. Friedrich appears much younger in this photograph than in the photographed titled *Krupp family with friends* even though we were told they were taken within a year of one another. Without a doubt Friedrich looks much older and heavier in weight in *Krupp Family with Friends*. He appears to have aged as much as 3-4 additional years than in the ThyssenKrupp website photograph.

Engelbertha appears to be about age eighteen or nineteen in this photograph, while Friedrich appears to look younger than her at about fifteen, or sixteen leading one to believe that Engelbertha was born before Friedrich. It is possible for someone to look younger than they actually are, but in this case we are looking at everything to explain Engelbertha's existence. One of the four responses she gave on public documents, Engelbertha said on at least one of them that she was born in 1854.[11] Is it plausible that Alfred Krupp had the Market Church records reflect it was Friedrich who was born in 1854, when in fact it was Engelbertha that was born in 1854? That would indicate that Friedrich was actually born in 1856. Remember, there were no paparazzi following the Krupp family during this time period like there is now. Their every move was not documented by the press.

If you look deeper to see who had more to lose by not getting it right you will discover the Krupp Archives does. With the secret well embedded in the minds of those who died long ago, the task of identifying this young girl sitting to the left of Bertha Krupp in the photograph *Krupp family with friends* falls not on the Bruch Archive, but the Krupp Archives. Why was a photograph of Clara Bruch taken without her husband, Max? Not only was he a friend of the family, his early musical career was financially supported by Alfred Krupp.[12] The outsider historians and archivists who oversee the Krupp and Bruch archives only know what appears on existing documents, books, and photographs in their care. The last thing they would ever think is that they were looking at a photograph of Engelbertha Krupp. They only know Friedrich to be the sole child of Alfred and Bertha. It was perfectly natural for them to consider other possible family friends sitting next to Bertha. Even the striking similarities between mother and daughter sitting next to each other apparently did not register at all at Villa Hugel because they did not have a clue that Engelbertha existed. The family's biggest secret died when Alfred, Bertha and Friedrich died and possibly when the Villa Hugel servants died too.

In the book *Pictures of Krupp: photography and history in the industrial age* the author stated there were, "noticeable gaps," in Krupp family photo albums that he, or the Krupp Archive, find difficult to explain.[13] The author goes on to say there were no special family albums during Alfred Krupp's time in Villa Hugel showing himself, Bertha and son Friedrich.[14] The fact that the albums seen today were put together after Alfred and Bertha's death seemed to support the idea that they did not care much for maintaining a photographic history of their marriage, nor of their son. Yet it was written in *Pictures of Krupp: photography and history in the industrial age* that Alfred went to the photographers often, and that he made it a point to professionally photograph the Stammhaus where he was born.[15] He even purposely maintained a large collection, or archive of his personal notes and letters to his family and staff at Krupp works[16] Why then did he not wish to keep a photographic history of his personal life that included his wife and child? This seems uncharacteristic of a man who unquestionably has a photographic preservationist mindset. The answer is that there were very likely early photographs of his children—both of them.

One can argue that from the noticeable gap in family photographs that Alfred Krupp had ordered his Villa Hugel staff to destroy all photographs showing his daughter appearing in them. There must have been many photographs showing Alfred, Bertha, Friedrich and Engelbertha appearing together because there are very few of them in existence today leading us to believe many were destroyed. Granted, I speak of photographs that are generally available for public view on the Internet and books by noted authors. It can be concluded that the photograph titled *Krupp family with Friends,* is the sole surviving photograph of Engelbertha Krupp spared most likely by an empathetic and courageous servant who knew what Alfred was doing was morally wrong. By hiding this specific photograph showing Engelbertha with her family, whoever took it had the presence of mind to think it would help to establish Engelbertha's true identity should the photograph resurface at a later date.

Chapter 16

THE FINAL ANALYSIS

I n closing, the evidence has been identified and presented to support the revelations told by Caroline Marchuck, Theodore Beebe, and Charles Stroebele. The photographic evidence also supports the fact that it is, in fact, Engelbertha Krupp that appears in a photograph with her parents and brother Friedrich. Many family photographs are thought to have been destroyed and altered, much like how Joseph Stalin and Adolf Hitler altered public posters and photographs to remove those who he had killed. Hitler used his military to destroy the very village—and church he was baptized in to remove all traces of his ancestry very much like how Alfred Krupp did with his daughter.

My family tree led me to seek out distant relatives. Those relative provided me with revelations. Those revelations led to the investigation. The investigation unearthed photographs and pieces of a puzzle that fell into place and unearth a family secret.

My investigation began in September 2008 when Caroline Marchuck, the granddaughter of Adolph Theodore Stroebele was told the story by Adolph about how John Stroebele had married Engelbertha Krupp, the daughter of the famous Krupp steel and armament industrialist in Essen, Germany under protest of the family.[1] After receiving a large sum of money from Alfred Krupp and hearing the words, "never darken my door again," Engelbertha and new husband John Stroebele immigrated to America.[2] This story helps explain and lends credibility to the story told by Theodore Beebe, and is corroborated by his cousin, Charles Stroebele that he was told that John and Engelbertha worked at the Berlin City Palace for Emperor Wilhelm I.[3] Wilhelm was a very close friend and confidant to Alfred Krupp.

It was Caroline Marchuck who informed me that it was not Engelbertha Arnold that John Stroebele had married, it was Engelbertha Krupp.[4] In a test to validate her credibility, additional facts Caroline provided were corroborated. These facts were not known by other members of my immediate family so they could not help me solve them.

The first fact was that John and Engelbertha brought with them to America a very large sum of money given to them by the Krupp family before they immigrated to America. The amount told to her presumably by her grandfather Adolph was $10,000.[5] One has to take into account that this is what was told to Adolph Stroebele by his father John Stroebele. However, it is believed Deutschmarks was most likely the currency given to them and when told the story by Adolph Stroebele he used dollars so whoever was listening would understand the currency exchange rate from German Marks to American dollars and not be confused by the word Deutschmarks. John Stroebele could have wanted to soften the reaction of his family to an even higher amount by using the lower amount of $10,000.

Determining approximately how much money was brought to America by Engelbertha and John Stroebele was done by calculating, in reverse order, by how much they already spent on necessities such as rent for their home, the family store, and the usual tax, food, clothing, medical expenses and utilities for a family of five. It was determined that they could not possibly have generated enough income to recover from the staggering cost to emigrate or sustain their lifestyle from the very first day Engelbertha arrived with her children in March 1883.[6] The remaining money that was brought by John Stroebele Sr. to Albany, New York when he went to live with his son and his family around the year 1915 produced a mysterious, impressive, and unexplainable trail of spending not possible given his son's low-paying employment history and his current occupation with the local railroad.[7] Caroline's credibility was becoming untouchable.

Caroline then stated that John Stroebele had a boot making business on Palisade Avenue in Jersey City near the hundred steps leading down into Hoboken from Palisade Avenue. That also proved to be correct as both John Stroebele's residence and business appeared in historic Jersey City address books right where Caroline said they were.[8] Caroline then stated that John Stroebele became friendly with a famous New York City jeweler whom he would talk with frequently in his store when the jeweler was in business in Jersey City.

It was learned through many hours of Internet research that Joseph Briggs was an artist that worked out of Jersey City for the famed New York City Jeweler Tiffany and Company.[9] Contact was made with Michael Burlingham, great-grandson of Louis Comfort Tiffany Jr. He confirmed that Tiffany indeed traveled to Jersey City frequently to conduct business with Joseph Briggs and may have interacted with his famous relative.[10] A fifth and final claim made by Caroline was corroborated and could only be done so by a person with the specific knowledge that was given to her by family members.

A fifth revelation of, "a city by the sea," by Caroline where John and Engelbertha had retreated to after leaving Villa Hugel, may never be determined unless German tax records surface indicating which city by the sea they stayed at. What is known is that the couple was employed by the Emperor of Prussia, Emperor Wilhelm I in Berlin before arriving in Sigmaringen to be married in August 1875 with Engelbertha being three-months pregnant.[11] It was doubtful their first child, John Stroebele Jr. was conceived inside the compound of Villa Hugel, possibly in the Krupp-provided housing John Stroebele occupied in Essen while employed by the Krupp family. One must also seriously consider that their first baby was conceived somewhere between Berlin and Sigmaringen, and even possibly in Sigmaringen, but without the aid of historic Sigmaringen address books to tell us exactly when they arrived there it would be difficult if not impossible to determine.

Engelbertha gave birth to four children in Sigmaringen. A baby girl, Walburga Bertha Stroebele died just five weeks after birth on November 4, 1877. [12] If you believe German naming conventions that say you should see first and middle names from the Stroebele family and the Arnold family, then look at the first and middle names of each of the three children you will notice that they all have the first and middle names exclusively from the Stroebele family indicating Engelbertha wanted no part of her family's past. True that a Josephine Arnold appeared as the American equivalent to Engelbertha's maid of honor at her wedding in Sigmaringen.[13] True also, that this Josephine was the sponsor at the baptisms of John Stroebele Jr. and Adolph Stroebele, but not at Otto's (it was Emma Kromer). If this so-called Josephine Arnold held such a dear place in the hearts of both John and Engelbertha, why then did they not at the least give their baby girl the middle name of Josephine? The answer is because this Josephine Arnold was most likely Emma Kromer the entire time. Baby John Joseph Stroebele Jr. was named after his father. Walburga Bertha was named after John's mother Walburga Staudinger, and Engelbertha. Adolph Theodore was named for the oldest brother of John Stroebele. Finally, baby Otto Wilhelm was named after the other brother of John Stroebele with the exception of the middle name Wilhelm (William).

Since the many birth records of the Stroebele family in Germany going back to the early-1700's do not contain the name Wilhelm, it was strongly suspected that Otto William Stroebele (1882-1928) was given his middle name in honor of Emperor Wilhelm I who secretly provided his parents refuge from Alfred Krupp and provided them employment in the Berlin City Palace after they left Villa Hugel in Essen. Otto William Stroebele passed his name onto one of his 13 children, Otto William Stroebele Jr. (1915-1996) also known as Otto "Dave" Stroebel.[14] Adolph Stroebele also passed this name onto his only son, William A. Stroebele, as did Gloria Stroebel Bekker who gave her son Paul William Bekker his middle name. Today, William Joseph Stroebel, son of the late Howard F. and Elizabeth "Betty" Stroebel carries that name on.

Engelbertha emigrated from Germany to America from the Port of Hamburg, which was not the normal port of embarkation taken by Southern Germans. The normal and common port was Le Havre, France. She had a good reason to divert north while her husband took the normal and expected route out of Southern Germany. It was believed she did this because she probably stopped in Essen one last time to say goodbye to either her mother, or her brother Friedrick before leaving Germany forever.

Not all those who emigrated from Wurttemberg near where John and Engelbertha lived appeared on the Wurttemberg immigration list.[15] In order to have appeared on the list signified that you received permission from your Emperor to emigrate. If later you decided that you did not like the country you emigrated to, you didn't always regain citizenship back and were considered a man without a country. Others preferred to emigrate under secrecy knowing they would have never been given permission to do so. Since John and Engelbertha do not appear on this list, it could be concluded that they chose to leave under secrecy for one or more reasons.

On the passenger list of the SS *Westphalia* on March 27, 1883, Engelbertha stated she was thirty-two years of age.[16] Doing the math would tell you she was born in 1851. The standard used in this book was 1854 for determining what year Engelbertha was born in against other documents detailing her age and date of birth, yet she gives different years that she was born on other documents.

Engelbertha and her three children came over in expensive second-class cabins.[17] The exorbitant ticket fare was uncharacteristic for the wife of a shoemaker who was expected to be a low-wage earner by way of his occupation. His family has no significant history of money. His father John Stroebele was a land owner and a low-wage earning teacher, hardly a career that would bring riches to his family.[18] John Stroebele's grandfather, Anton Stroebele, was a wagoner (driver)—also a low-wage job. Both of John Stroebele's parents died in 1848 when he was only three years of age and they at thirty-three and twenty-nine years of age, respectively. Despite a lack of money in his family line, John and Engelbertha Stroebele lived quite comfortably in Jersey City from approximately 1883 to 1915.

One of the strongest pieces of evidence of how much money John Stroebele Sr. must have possessed was when his boot making business failed. Why it failed is not nearly as important as what he did next. When his cash flow from customers dried up in his boot making store, his business failed. He apparently had more than enough money to immediately open a fully-stocked saloon.[19] The establishment of this saloon was uncharacteristic of a man whose business has failed. His actions told us he did not have a shortage of cash in which to open this saloon.

When immigrants (especially German and Irish) moved from residence to residence and store to store, it was usually because the owner of the building or home raised their rent based on what the owner's perception of the immigrant's income. What the owners saw convinced them that the immigrants could afford higher rents. John and Engelbertha moved their residence and business a total of 13 times from 1883 to 1915. It can be argued that something the owners saw convinced them that John and Engelbertha could and would pay the higher rent. Although they had more than enough to pay the increase, it could have been the principal of the matter that compelled them to move, or possibly that their neighbors became too curious about the family and moving would eliminate any relationship their neighbors had tried to establish with the Stroebele family.

Evidence of the crosses and bibles in every Protestant Church in Essen with the words, "personal property of Krupp," stamped on each of them was a barometer of the power, influence, and control Krupp wielded over the churches and even the government of Essen enabling him to order the Protestant Church of Germany to remove and destroy any trace of his daughter's birth records.[20] He had the motive, power and will to do this. Ironically, my great-great-grandfather was also described as a militant atheist.[21]

Two things happened when Alfred Krupp passed the entire Krupp inheritance to his son Friedrich. First, Friedrich inherited the entire Krupp industrial empire. Second, he broke German law when his biological daughter, Engelbertha received nothing. This is considered a crime and not permissible by German law.[22] Cut and dry. Case closed. Although Engelbertha received a large sum of money in which she transported to America, it was a transaction under the table. It was hush money—a bribe. Let me end by saying it was probably very tiny in comparison to what she was legally entitled to—a half of the Krupp Empire, but consensus is growing that she may be the sole heiress.

Two photographs taken of Emma Kromer in Newark and New York City provide key evidence that she traveled from Germany to visit her brother on at least two occasions, yet no record of arrival for an Emma Kromer with a date of birth near 1846 was found in the Ellis Island or Castle Garden databases. Because of this, it was believed that she too possibly used an alias because her sister-in-law was a Krupp and she was requested by her brother John Stroebele Sr. to do so to hide any trail back to his wife and the Krupp family in Essen.

We know from looking at John Stroebele's State of New Jersey death certificate that he did not want his parents' names known in spite of the fact that he himself gave his parents' names to St. John's Church officials who entered it in his marriage record.[23] Why then did John Stroebele Sr. purposely withhold that information from his children? The answer is because he did not want his children to find family information on him back in Germany because all roads lead to Essen and the Krupp dynasty. Why go through that trouble when he himself identified Engelbertha's parents on her State of New Jersey Death Certificate as Joseph Arnold and Barbara Biedermann?[24] John Stroebele was crafty. We see it here because he knew it would be highly suspicious if both he and his wife did not know the names of their parents. It is believed he used someone else's names for Engelbertha's parents to avoid heightening their children's suspicions. For some unknown reason, while he was probably still in Germany, he selected the names of Joseph Arnold and Barbara Biedermann. Yes, these names were listed in the St. John's birth book, and could be the names of real living people, you cannot escape the fact that there was also another Barbara Biedermann who lived just thirty miles from John and Engelbertha Stroebele in Assmannshardt, Baden-Wurttemberg, and she was married to an Anton Stroebele.[25] Their son Joseph Stroebele was the Mayor of Sigmaringen in 1865![26] Joseph's daughter Aloysia Stroebele immigrated to Butler, and became a pioneer in naturopathic medicine just 37 miles from Jersey City! Was this all a coincidence? Was this John Stroebele's relative?

Alfred Krupp has in the past demonstrated that he was willing and able to banish and disinherit members of his family. Engelbertha was not the first child of his to have inheritance used against her. Alfred Krupp demonstrated that he was violent, abusive, manipulative, cunning, vengeful, and extremely spiteful. He willfully behaved this way to his immediate family and business associates. In the many incidents highlighted here, Alfred Krupp was more than willing and capable in banishing his only daughter and cutting her off from her rightful inheritance. We can argue that the only reason why he did not disinherit wife Bertha is because she would have revealed what he did to

Engelbertha and his empire and personal aspects of his life would have be severely impacted under such heavy weight. Whatever the reason, he chose not to disinherit his wife. Daughter Engelbertha, under German law could not run the vast empire because she was a woman, so she was no good to the family in Alfred's eyes and was expendable.

Alfred Krupp harbored such disdain toward famous German musician and conductor Max Bruch, but reluctantly financed his early schooling and career at the insistence of wife Bertha who was the cousin of Bruch's wife Clara. Alfred Krupp made statements that Bruch was completely wasting his time devoting his life to music and was, "leading an utter pointless existence," in doing so.[27] Then how was it that Alfred Krupp reportedly had first met wife Bertha in a theatre in Cologne in 1853 before he proposed to her? Is this the same man that said musicians lead an utterly pointless existence and are wasting their time? The point I am making is that it was doubtful Alfred would have spontaneously gone alone as the Krupp Archives says to attend a performance at an unnamed theatre for a performance that was not identified.[28] Why would Alfred Krupp attend an utterly pointless performance that would certainly waste his time? The story of how he met Bertha just does not fit into his character.

A clearer picture perhaps is beginning to appear that Alfred never went to a theater performance and if this unidentified performance (neither Bertha nor Alfred could remember?) in an unidentified theatre was to be made public, a timeframe could be established from when the performance ran against the date Alfred and Bertha were wed in 1853. Chances are good that you would find a discrepancy in the Krupp Archives' story about how the two met, when and where. In one of Alfred's many letters to wife Bertha he often used futile attempts at terms of endearment. Of these is one that immediately draws our attention and puts a white hot spotlight on it. From my prospective it's a bombshell. It is Alfred's words to his wife Bertha, "Dear best of Berthas."[29] It is revealing in the sense that it is plural and implies there is more than one Bertha living in the house and that one Bertha behaves well while the other does not. After Engelbertha Krupp was married and immigrated to America in 1883 she went by Bertha, not her birth name Engelbertha. It tells us for the first time there is another Bertha in the family—in the very same house. It also tells us that wife Bertha has perhaps also grown weary of her daughter's non-compliant behavior toward her father. She may in fact been a thorn in both her parent's side. This would explain why Bertha initially did not take sides with her daughter and thought it best if she spent some time away from the dynasty's shadow and clear her mind in regards to marrying John Stroebele Sr.

Alfred Krupp expected and demanded absolute loyalty from his work-force.[30] It could be a true statement that these expectations transcended to his own family—daughter especially. Workers at the Krupp works had their expectations spelled out for them by Herr Krupp so there was no misunder-standing as to who was in charge and the importance in their work.[31] It is also very likely that he used the same approach with his wife and children. Friedrich complied out of design, but Engelbertha was incapable to comply out of that same design. It is quite apparent that Engelbertha did not buy into her father's philosophy and paid dearly. Alfred had secretly ordered the passive observation of his workers on the job—not because he suspected any-thing.[32] He believed that he should be able to detect any uncooperative per-sonalities who may raise objections at a future time. If Alfred did this same thing at home it surely would have galvanized Engelbertha into objectionable behavior toward her father. Alfred demonstrated just how cold and unfor-giving he could be toward a relative citing his coldness toward his cousin Friedrich Solling as discussed earlier. This story makes us believe Alfred was more than willing and capable of doing the same to his daughter by banishing her right to the grave.[33]

Engelbertha hid both her true identity, and pregnancy from St. John's Catholic Church in Sigmaringen. We know this because Engelbertha and John were married on August 31, 1875, and she gave birth to their first child, John Joseph Stroebele Jr. on February 16, 1876, just six months later and three months shy of a full-term baby.[34] It is believed that Engelbertha lied to St. John's Catholic Church when asked if she was Catholic (she was Protestant) and concealed from them the fact she was pregnant. She has established her-self as dishonest right from the start in Sigmaringen. Why should we take her on her word on the documents with her name on them and described in this book? Why lie about her last name and lie about her pregnancy? It was essential that she be married before a full-blown pregnancy would be impossible to hide from the eyes of any church and secondly, she certainly did not want her first child born out of wedlock. It is very unusual that the block on her church marriage record stating her place of birth was left blank, implying she did not know, or the church official overlooked it. Playing the devil's advocate, let's assume she did not know where she was born. Why not enter unknown? St. John's Church stated they had a birth record for an Engelbertha Arnold born in Sigmaringen on June 13, 1851, to Joseph Arnold and Barbara Biedermann. If St. John's Church in Sigmaringen knew where Engelbertha Arnold was born and had a birth record for her, why didn't Engelbertha herself know on her wedding day?[35] There is a major conflict here. If Engelbertha knew what her parents' names were as she stated, why then did she not know where she was born? St. John's did. It makes absolutely no sense. It is almost as if her marriage record existed before her birth record and as if the birth record was created in 1875 for a woman reportedly born in 1854. It is quite possible this birth record was created after the fact with pressure (and possibly money) from someone in a position of power, wealth, or both.

Once settled in Jersey City, Engelbertha begins giving incorrect years of birth for her and husband John in an effort to keep anyone from knowing details about them and their past in Germany. When she does this, Engelbertha is demonstrating how difficult it is to remember a lie. In law enforcement, the reason why police will question a suspect over and over again is because they want to see if their story changes. If it does, it tells the police that this suspect most likely did not experience the story they have told them—they fabricated it. Engelbertha is asked her age and date of birth 3-4 times over a span of 27 years and her story has changed. She gives an incorrect birth month and year for husband John in 1900, but gets it right ten years later because it is too hard to remember a lie, but easy to remember what is really true.

On her 1900 US Census, Engelbertha incorrectly states she and John immigrated in 1885, but amazingly ten years later (and 10 years older at age fifty-eight) on the 1910 Census she gets it right by saying they immigrated in

1882 and 1883, respectively.[36] Engelbertha was either tired of lying or can't remember what she told the last Census counter in 1900. It is more believable that she had trouble remembering what she told the last census taker since it was not based on a truthful event. We know this to be true because she admits for the first time that on the 1910 Census she is the mother of five children, not three like she stated on the 1900 Census.[37] The truth has finally come out.

There is no evidence by way of deed or mortgage that exists in either of the couple's names in Hudson County where they lived for 33 years. Therefore, it is believed that the couple never purchased any homes or took out a mortgage because a deed or mortgage would have revealed they had money, started a trail that could lead to Germany, and the Krupp dynasty in Essen. Besides, they had a significant amount of money and renting did not present a financial hardship and allowed them to exist under a cloak of anonymity.

Baptismal records for Karl Stroebele, Engelbertha's only child to be born in America in 1884, show he was first given the middle name, "Frederick," the American translation of, "Friedrich," the name of her brother in Germany. A second baptismal record shows it being changed to, "Karl Anton Engelberth Stroebele," Did Engelbertha name her child after her brother, Friedrich Krupp, in Germany?

There was evidence by way of deeds, but no mortgages (meaningful that is), to the many homes and pieces of property purchased by the Albany Stroebele family clearly indicating that the remaining fortune brought from Germany by John Stroebele was transported with him from Jersey City and was being spent with, or without his consent by his eldest son John Stroebele Jr.

Approximately one hundred thirty-six years has passed since Engelbertha was banished and disinherited by her father, Alfred Krupp. All the major players involved from Bertha and Friedrich to the many house servants present that day have long since died. No doubt they were all compelled by Alfred to turn a blind-eye at the cost of losing their inheritance, jobs, pensions, security, and possibly their personal safety and the safety of their families. Engelbertha was the only child of Alfred and Bertha Krupp to give birth to sons—three of them, a key requirement for inheriting and operating the Krupp Empire.

Friedrich Krupp raised two girls. How history will determine this will be left in the hands of German scholars to decide. Engelbertha was forced to leave her family in Germany because of her marriage to John Stroebele. If she had been permitted by Alfred Krupp to raise her three sons John, Adolph, and Otto Stroebele peacefully in Essen in the shadow of her parents and Friedrich, there would have been no need for an arranged marriage between Friedrich's daughter Bertha Krupp and Gustav because Friedrich's daughter Bertha would not have inherited the Krupp Empire. Engelbertha had the most eligible children (all males) to manage and operate the Krupp works. It has been told through intimate family stories that these three sons of Engelbertha were kind, compassionate and respectful family men who did not harm a single sole during their lifetimes. The absence of the Stroebele name from the Krupp landscape perhaps altered history forever. Alfried Krupp von Bohlen und Halbach gave Adolf Hitler's Third Reich immense firepower allowing the dynasty's war machine to reach as far across the globe as it did. It is unlikely that Engelbertha would have continued munitions production and would have steered the firm to more peaceful production.

The only possible way this story could have made it out into the light of day as it did was by John Stroebele Sr. to his son Adolph then told to Adolph's granddaughter, Caroline Marchuck. There is no evidence that tells us that Engelbertha had told anyone about her banishment. It was her husband John Stroebele. Did Emma Kromer tell her family in Sigmaringen? Records in German tell us none of her three children ever married nor had children. But the hope is that someone may come forward as a result of this book. There is a very long and incriminating trail of evidence supporting the existence of Engelbertha Krupp all the way from Villa Hugel in Essen, to Jersey City to Albany and Monticello in upstate New York. Alfred Krupp may have taken his daughter's existence from her, but he was never able to take her soul. Her spirit lives on in the many surviving members of her family across these United States.

EPILOGUE

The discovery of this unrecorded banishment in the Krupp dynasty may make the list of the most challenging problems for the Alfried Krupp von Bohlen und Halbach Foundation and ThyssenKrupp AG since World War II. How it treats these revelations may define their moral compass and character. A full accounting of all holdings in their archive must be made accessible to the public for examination for more information as to the life of Engelbertha Krupp—who was to be the rightful and legal heiress to the Krupp works and Germany's true Cannon Queen.

ACKNOWLEDGEMENTS

The author would like to thank those in the United States, Germany, and the United Kingdom who graciously provided information, records and documentation used in this book. Although they did not know the historic impact of their contributions at the time, they can feel secure in the knowledge that their willingness to help in this historic book helped redefine German, and perhaps world history. To my Aunt Gloria Bekker, who was severely injured in an automobile accident near Los Angeles in 1966. The accident left her unable to care for herself, let alone husband Peter and her three young boys: Peter—13, Paul—11, and Frederick—4 months, who meant the world to her. She would spend more than half her life in a nursing home unable to comprehend the outside world as we know it. Having never met my Aunt Gloria, or any of the Bekker family, hearing the news of her death in 2007 compelled me to learn more about the aunts and uncles I had never known. Having never visited her at the nursing home in Croton-on-Hudson, New York, I was overcome with guilt. It was while I was searching for my ancestry that I found a dynasty. If it were not for Aunt Gloria, I would not have a reason to write this book. I give my thanks to the late author William R. Manchester for writing in such intimate detail about my Krupp relatives. John Manchester, Caroline Marchuck, Theodore Beebe, Charles M. Stroebele John Stephen Stroebele Lillian Goldberg, Christopher Fifield,

Michael Burlingham, Sigmaringen Mayor Dr. Daniel Rapp, Karl-Heinz Berger—St. John's Catholic Church, Stefan Koppleman—Protestant Church of Essen, Schloss Sigmaringen, Timo Hartmann, Sigmaringen City Archives, Jennifer Bartoli, ThyssenKrupp AG/Alfried Krupp von Bohlen und Halbach Foundation & Archive, Anna Stroebel Barton, Dorothy Stroebel Borchers, Greg Harlow, Peter O.E. Bekker, Jr. Nancy Stroebel Ahlers, John J. Hallanan III, Peter Schuck, Xenia Wohlschiess, Derek and Michelle Gonzales, Marge Spille, Beverly G. Kirby-McDonough, John Engle, and Cynthia Harris from the Jersey City Free Public Library. Special thanks to my sister, Jennifer Stroebel, for funding this endeavor. The Blanche and Irving Laurie Music Library, Mabel Smith Douglass Library, Eastern and Western Branch of the Monmouth County Library, Office of the Hudson County Registrar, Sullivan County Clerk's Office, Albany County Clerk's Office, New Jersey State Archives, Sigmaringen City Archives, Freiberg Archives, Max Bruch Archives, Eatontown, New Jersey Family History Center of The Church of Jesus Christ of Ladder-day Saints, Familysearch.org, Castlegarden.org, Ancestry.com, the army of genealogists on the following Rootsweb.com email lists: NJHudson, Baden-Wurttemberg, Roots, PrussiaRoots, German-Military, NYAlbany, NYSullivan, and German-Military.

Appendix I

STROEBELE GENEALOGY

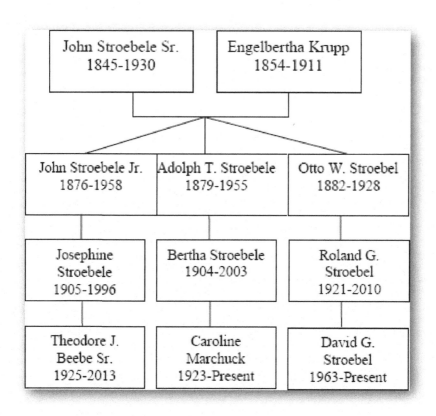

Appendix II

CHARLES M. STROEBELE
GENEALOGY

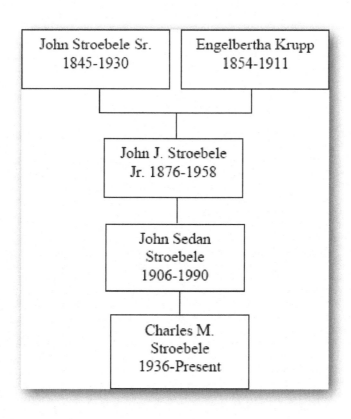

John Stroebele Sr.
1845-1930

Engelbertha Krupp
1854-1911

John J. Stroebele
Jr. 1876-1958

John Sedan
Stroebele
1906-1990

Charles M.
Stroebele
1936-Present

Appendix III

KRUPP GENEALOGY

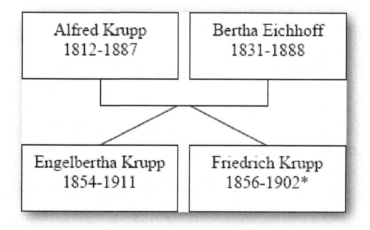

*Author suggests Engelbertha Krupp was born sooner than brother Friedrich.

Appendix IV

STROEBELE-KRUPP
COMPARISON GENEALOGY

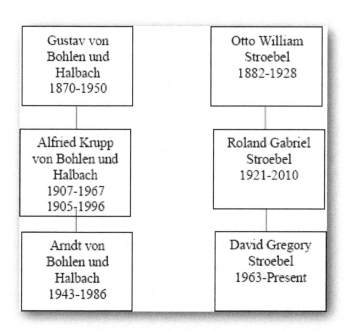

(location where author David Stroebel falls on his family tree versus the Krupp family tree)

Apendix V

CHRONOLOGY

1587   The first Krupp—Arndt Krupp—settles in Essen.

1599   Plague in Essen makes Arndt wealthy.

1703   Arnold Krupp becomes second Mayor of Essen.

1811   Friedrich Krupp establishes Krupp family steel foundry.

1812   Birth of Alfred Felix Alwyn Krupp in Essen.

1831   Birth of Bertha Eichhoff in Cologne.

1845   Birth of John Joseph Stroebele Sr.
in Veringendorf, Baden-Wurttemberg.

1846   Birth of Emma Stroebele in Ostrach, Baden-Wurttemberg.

1851   Documented birth year of Engelbertha Krupp in Sigmaringen.

1853   Documented marriage of Alfred Krupp and Bertha Eichhoff in Essen.

1854   Documented birth of Friedrich Krupp in Essen.

1868   Engelbertha Krupp appears in family photograph with parents Alfred and Bertha Krupp along with brother Friedrich.

1870   John Stroebele Sr. attends baptism of nephew Eugene John Kromer in Sigmaringen.

1870   John Stroebele Sr. serves as a Prussian Army Officer during the Franco-Prussian War.

1871   Undocumented year John Stroebele Sr. was thought to have arrived at Villa Hugel for work as a bootblack.

1873   Financial Panic of '73 hits Krupp works.

1874   Engelbertha Krupp is banished and disinherited from Krupp industrial dynasty.

John and Engelbertha leave Villa Hugel for unknown city along the coast of Germany.

1875   John and Engelbertha arrive in Sigmaringen and marry at St. John's Catholic Church.

1876   Birth of John Joseph Stroebele Jr. to John and Engelbertha Stroebele in Sigmaringen, Baden-Wurttemberg.

1879   Birth of Adolph Stroebele to John and Engelbertha Stroebele in Sigmaringen.

1882   Engelbertha travels to Villa Hugel and receives large sum of money from her father, Alfred Krupp.

Birth of Otto William Stroebel to John and Engelbertha Stroebele in Sigmaringen.

John Stroebele emigrates from Sigmaringen three months ahead of wife Engelbertha.

1883   Engelbertha emigrates from Sigmaringen via the Port of Hamburg with sons John, Adolph, and Otto.

John Stroebele Sr. establishes a boot making business in Jersey City, New Jersey.

1887   Alfred Krupp dies in Essen at age 75.

1888   Death of Bertha Krupp in Essen at age 57.

1890   Birth of Julia Anne Hauser in Jersey City.

1892   Emma Kromer makes first of two US visits.

1897   John Stroebele Sr. opens saloon after boot making business falters.

1898   John Stroebele Jr. enlists in the US Army during Spanish-American War.

1901   First blueprints for Krupp German U-boat Program drawn.

1902   Friedrich Alfried Krupp reportedly dies from a stroke.

Daughter Bertha inherits entire Krupp Empire.

1904   Emma Kromer makes second US visit.

1906   Bertha marries Gustav von Bohlen und Halbach.

Marriage of Otto William Stroebel and Julia Anne Hauser in Hoboken.

Engelbertha Krupp Stroebele appears in photograph taken in Jersey City with John Stroebele Sr. and Emma Kromer.

Birth of John Sedan Stroebele in Queens, New York.

1907   Birth of Alfried Krupp von Bohlen und Halbach in Essen.

1911   Engelbertha Stroebele dies from a stroke at age 59 in Union City, New Jersey.

1915   John Stroebele Jr. arrives in Albany, New York.

1921   Birth of Roland G. Stroebel in Jersey City.

1923   John and Linda Stroebele begin pattern of unexplained spending.

1928   Death of Otto William Stroebel in Jersey City.

1930   Death of John Stroebele Sr. in Jersey City.

1934   Hitler decree names Gustav, *Leader of the Economy.*

Adolf Hitler visits the Krupp works in Essen.

1937   Mussolini visits the Krupp Works in Essen.

1931   Alfried Krupp von Bohlen und Halbach joins the Nazi SS.

1933   Krupp works provides financial backing to Adolf Hitler.

Title of *Furher of Industry,* bestowed onto Gustav.

1940   First of six children of Otto and Julia Stroebel enter US military service for World War II.

1942   James E. Beebe enters US military service for World War II.

1943   Adolf Hitler passes Lex Krupp Decree.

1943   John Sedan Stroebele son of John and Linda Stroebele enter US military service for World War II.

1943   First of two sons of Josephine L. and James E. Beebe enter US military service for World War II.

1944   Number of slave labors by Alfried Krupp number at 100,000.

1946   Krupp factories dismantled by allies.

1948   Nuremberg Tribunal convicts Alfried Krupp von Bohlen und Halbach of war crimes.

US Army Lieutenant Otto "Dave" Stroebel oversees war crimes prisoners at Nuremberg Prison.

1950   Death of Gustav Krupp von Bohlen und Halbach Bluhnbach, Austria.

1955   Death of Adolph Stroebele in Secaucus.

1957   Death of Bertha Krupp in Essen.

1958   Death of John Stroebele Jr. in Albany

1963   Birth of David G. Stroebel.

1886   Death of Arndt Krupp von Bohlen und Halbach, last namesake of Krupp dynasty.

2007   Death of Gloria Bekker in Croton-on-Hudson.
        David Stroebel begins research on Stroebel family tree.

2008   Story of Engelbertha Krupp is conveyed to David Stroebel.

2009   Photographs of Engelbertha Krupp are discovered.

Appendix VI

REVELATIONS

Revelations communicated to author David G. Stroebel directly and indirectly supporting the banishment theory of Engelbertha Krupp Stroebele

Revelation 1. From Roland Stroebel (father of David Stroebel), late 1980s: When asked from where in Germany our Stroebel family originated, came the answer, "Essen."

Revelation 2. From Mary Stroebel (mother of David Stroebel), early 1990s: When asked from where in Germany our Stroebel family originated, came the answer, "Essen."

Revelation 3. From Theodore J. Beebe Sr (son of Josephine Stroebele Beebe Adriance) July 2008 - John and Engelbertha worked for Kaiser Wilhelm I at the Berlin City Palace. John worked as a boot black and Engelbertha worked in the kitchen. She enjoyed making omelets.

Revelations 4-8, From Caroline Marchuck, age 86 (granddaughter of Adolph Stroebele):

Revelation 4. John Stroebele Sr. married Engelbertha Krupp from the famous steel and munitions manufacturer in Essen and Engelbertha's parents did not approve of this marriage and threatened her with disinheritance if she proceeded.

Revelation 5. After departing Villa Hugel for the last time, John and Engelbertha stayed for a short time at, "a city by the sea," somewhere in Germany. Caroline could not remember the name of the city.

Revelation 6. John and Engelbertha brought $10,000 to the United States that was given to them by Alfred Krupp with these specific words: "never darken my door again." The correct denomination was Deutsche Mark. David Stroebel and Theodore Beebe estimated it to be between $2 million and $6 million that was received from Alfred Krupp that still exists today (from 1883) in the form of a trust fund for Charles and John Stroebele of Scotia and Albany, New York.

Revelation 7. John Stroebele Sr. operated a shoemaking business on Palisade Avenue in Jersey City, New Jersey, USA after he immigrated in 1882. This was corroborated via historic address directories on Ancestory.com.

Revelation 8. There was a famous jeweler from New York that became friendly with John Stroebele Sr. because they frequently rented a room next to his business in Jersey City. The jeweler was identified as Louis Comfort Tiffany, Jr.

Revelation 9. From Charles M. Stroebele Scotia, New York. John and Engelbertha Stroebele told their children their family roots were located in Sedan, France (debunked). Genealogy records prove the Stroebele family origins stretched back to 1736 in Ostrach, Baden-Wurttemberg, Germany, not Sedan, France.

Revelations 10-14 were made by Charles M. Stroebele of Scotia, New York and support the trail of money discovered first in Albany c.1923 being spent by John and Engelbertha's son, John Stroebele Jr. He began accessing the bank account of his elderly father when his father moved in with him in Albany in 1915. Father and son both had the same identical name.

Revelation 10. Land records obtained by author David Stroebel show John Stroebele Jr. began collecting the first of six homes in Albany and Monticello, New York, in 1923 with the money given to John and Engelbertha from Alfred Krupp.

Revelation 11. John Stroebele Jr. paid an $89,000 hospital bill c. 1950 in Albany for his wife in cash. Corroborated by elderly cousin Charles M. Stroebele.

Revelation 12. John Stroebele Jr. withdrew approximately $10,000 every two weeks from the bank to cash the paychecks of railroad workers at the family bar and grill in Albany. This was debunked by his cousin who stated there weren't enough railroad workers at the family bar and grill to warrant that much money withdrawn from the bank.

Revelation 13. Charles Stroebele stated his father, John Sedan Stroebele easily paid gambling debts in excess of $16,000 by asking a young Charles Stroebele who was twelve years of age to fetch the money from the rafters in the family basement.

Revelation 14. Charles M. Stroebele also stated that when his bank notified him they were closing his account due to failure to maintain the minimum amount, his grandfather, John Stroebele Jr. marched down to the bank with young Charles in tow demanding that if they closed his grandson's account, they could close, "all his accounts," (plural) indicating he had more than one account. Back then, the FDIC only insured accounts with less than $45,000 c. 1947.

Revelation 15. Judith Linde (great-niece of Engelbertha Krupp): Revelation passed down from Engelbertha or John Stroebele that the Stroebele family was related to Wilhelm I, Emperor of Germany. Wilhelm aided John and Engelbertha by providing them shelter and work at the Berlin palace. They, in-turn gave their one son the middle name, Wilhelm, upon baptism. It was a name that was never used by the family going back to the year 1736, or at least not properly recorded.

CHAPTER NOTES

Chapter 1

1. Manchester, William (1968). *The Arms of Krupp: 1587 - 1968*. Boston: Little, Brown and Company, 23.

2. Manchester, *Arms of Krupp*, 25.

3. Woodbridge Michaelis, Kate; Michaelis, Ortho E; Monthaye, E. *Alfred Krupp: a sketch of his life and work: after the German of Victor Niemeyer*, 3.

4. Manchester, *Arms of Krupp*, 30.

5. Manchester, *Arms of Krupp*, 30.

6. Manchester, *Arms of Krupp*, 34.

7. Manchester, *Arms of Krupp*, 40.

8. Manchester, *Arms of Krupp*, 42.

9. Manchester, *Arms of Krupp*, 42.

10. Muller, Friedrich Carl Georg, *Krupp's steel works*, 39.

11. Manchester, *Arms of Krupp*, 69.

12. Manchester, *Arms of Krupp*, 119.

13. Manchester, *Arms of Krupp*, 152.

14. Manchester, *Arms of Krupp*, 48.

15. Manchester, *Arms of Krupp*, 48.

16. Manchester, *Arms of Krupp*, 182.

17. Manchester, *Arms of Krupp*, 209.

18. Manchester, *Arms of Krupp*, 209.

19. Manchester, *Arms of Krupp*, 182.

20. Manchester, *Arms of Krupp*, 190.

21. Manchester, *Arms of Krupp*, 190.

22. Manchester, *Arms of Krupp*, 182.

23. Manchester, *Arms of Krupp*, 182.

24. Manchester, *Arms of Krupp*, 192.

25. Manchester, *Arms of Krupp*, 194.

26. Manchester, *Arms of Krupp*, 194.

27. Manchester, *Arms of Krupp*, 194.

28. Manchester, *Arms of Krupp*, 194.

29. Manchester, *Arms of Krupp*, 207.

30. Manchester, *Arms of Krupp*, 354.

31. Manchester, *Arms of Krupp*, 202.

32. Manchester, *Arms of Krupp*, 238.

33. Stanford School of Medicine Stroke Center. "Stroke Prevention." Stanford School of Medicine. http://strokecenter.stanford.edu/guide/prevention. html. 26 August 2009.

34. Stanford School of Medicine Stroke Center. "Stroke Prevention." Stanford School of Medicine. http://strokecenter.stanford.edu/guide/prevention. html. 26 August 2009.

35. Manchester, *Arms of Krupp*, 246.

36. Manchester, *Arms of Krupp*, 8.

37. Manchester, *Arms of Krupp*, 11.

38. Manchester, *Arms of Krupp*, 450.

39. Manchester, *Arms of Krupp*, 562, 866.

40. Manchester, *Arms of Krupp*, 453, 509, 538.

41. Manchester, *Arms of Krupp*, 657.

42. Manchester, *Arms of Krupp*, 679.

43. *Trial of the Major War Criminals Before the International Military Tribunal, Nuremberg*. 14 November 1945-October 1946, Volume 36, 522. Otto David Stroebel, Headquarters Command, European Command, World War II Compiled Military Service Records, National Archives, Washington, D.C.

44. Arlaine Robb, "Re: Book on Stroebels." Email message to author, 11 August 2009.

Chapter 2

1. Bertha Stroebele SS *Westphalia* Passenger Manifest, 27 March 1883. Online database castlegarden.org. Passenger and Crew Lists of Vessels Arriving at New York, 1855 to 1890.

2. Bertha Stroebele SS *Westphalia* Passenger Manifest, 27 March 1883. Online database castlegarden.org. Passenger and Crew Lists of Vessels Arriving at New York, 1855 to 1890.

3. Johann Stroebke, SS *Zeeland* Passenger Manifest, 5 December 1882. Online database castlegarden.org. Passenger and Crew Lists of Vessels Arriving at New York, 1855 to 1890.

4. Johann Stroebke, SS *Zeeland* Passenger Manifest, 5 December 1882. Online database castlegarden.org. Passenger and Crew Lists of Vessels Arriving at New York, 1855 to 1890.

5. Manchester, *Arms of Krupp*, 131.

6. Jesus Christ of Ladder-day Saints film, 896138, Sigmaringen, Baden-Wurttemberg Kirchenbuch taufen (Catholic Church book of baptisms) 1790-1868, entry 39.

7. Manchester, *Arms of Krupp*, 204.

8. Marriage record for Emma Stroebele and Eugene Kromer, 10 August 1869, St. John's Catholic Church Register, Sigmaringen, Baden-Wurttemberg, Germany.

9. Tenfelde, Klaus (1994). *Pictures of Krupp: photography and history in the industrial age*, Philip Wilson Publishers, 209.

10. Tenfelde, Klaus (1994). *Pictures of Krupp: photography and history in the industrial age.* 209.

11. Krupp Historical Archive. "Alfried Krupp von Bohlen und Halbach Foundation Krupp Historical Archive - Archive history." ThyssenKrupp website. http://www.thyssenkrupp.com/en/konzern/geschichte_archive_k1_2.html. 24 December 2009.

12. Thyssenkrupp. "Alfried Krupp von Bohlen und Halbach Foundation Krupp Historical Archive - Archive history." Thyssenkrupp.com. thyssenkrupp.com/en/konzern/geschichte_archive_k1_2.html. 24 December 2009.

13. Caroline Marchuck, telephone conversation with author, 18 September 2008.

14. Manchester, *Arms of Krupp*, 182.

Chapter 3

1. 1900 U.S. Federal Census (population schedule), Jersey City, Hudson County, New Jersey, Dwelling 115, Family 155, John Stroebele household," jpeg image, (online: The Generations Network, Inc., 2001) [Digital scan of original records in the National Archives, Washington, DC], subscription database, <http://www.ancestry.com>, accessed 16 December 2009.

2. 1910 U.S. Federal Census (population schedule), Jersey City, Hudson County, New Jersey, Dwelling 198, Family 94, John Stroebele household," jpeg image, (online: The Generations Network, Inc., 2001) [Digital scan of original records in the National Archives, Washington, DC], subscription database, <http://www.ancestry.com>, accessed 16 December 2009.

4. 1930 U.S. Federal Census (population schedule), Jersey City, Hudson County, New Jersey, Dwelling 114, Family 183, Julia Stroebel household," jpeg image, (online: The Generations Network, Inc., 2001) [Digital scan of original records in the National Archives, Washington, DC], subscription database, <http://www.ancestry.com>, accessed 2 May 2009.

5. Marriage record for Emma Stroebele and William Engelbrecht, (date), St. John's Catholic Church Register, Secaucus, New Jersey.

6. "Boy Drowns on Sled." *Hudson Evening Newspaper*, 18 January 1922, 1.

7. Certificate of Death: William Stroebele. Filed 20 March 1922. State of New Jersey, Bureau of Vital Statistics, Certificate of Record of Death, Reg. No. 1123. Informant: Mrs. Helene Stroebele [nee Magdalena Lamprecht, mother of deceased], Secaucus, New Jersey.

8. Caroline Marchuck, telephone conversation with author, 18 September 2008.

9. Caroline Marchuck, telephone conversation with author, 18 September 2008.

10. Caroline Marchuck, telephone conversation with author, 18 September 2008.

11. Caroline Marchuck, telephone conversation with author, 18 September 2008.

12. "Boy on Sled Drowns," *Hudson Evening News*, 18 January 1922.

Chapter 4

1. Deed from The Hoboken Building and Loan Association to Jefferson Trucking and Rigging Co., Inc., Hudson County Deed Book 1578, 180-1, Registrar's Office, Jersey City, New Jersey.

2. Certificate of Death: Otto Stroebel. Filed 7 November 1928. State of New Jersey, Bureau of Vital Statistics, Certificate of Record of Death, Reg. No. 13771. Informant: Fred Stroebel, [son of deceased], Jersey City, New Jersey.

3. Supreme Court of New Jersey. Stroebel v. Jefferson Trucking and Rigging Company, Inc. 11 A.2d 297 No. 249 (1940).

4. Patricia Dawley, telephone conversation with author, 21 October 2008.

5. Rootsweb, "Social Security Death Index."

6. *Genealogical history of Hudson and Bergen counties, New Jersey*, Cornelius Burnham Harvey, NJ genealogy Publishing Co. New York, 590.

7. Obituary for Emma Engelbrecht, Lakehurst, N.J. *Asbury Park Press*, (30 May 1991), C8.

8. Caroline Marchuck, telephone conversation with author, 18 September 2008.

9. Wojciech Plosa, Head of Archive, The State Museum Auschwitz-Birkenau in Oswiecim, "Re: your request for Krupp list," email message to author, 27 August 2009.

10. Caroline Marchuck, telephone conversation with author, 18 September 2008.

11. Caroline Marchuck, telephone conversation with author, 18 September 2008.

12. Caroline Marchuck, telephone conversation with author, 18 September 2008.

13. Caroline Marchuck, telephone conversation with author, 18 September 2008.

14. Caroline Marchuck, telephone conversation with author, 18 September 2008.

15. WH H. Boyd Gopsill (1883-84), Jersey City, and Hoboken Directory, 436.

16. Burlingham, Michael J. "Re: Louis Tiffany Story on NYTimes.com." Email to the author, 25 December 2008.

Chapter 5

1. Theodore J. Beebe Sr. telephone conversation with author. 18 July 2008.

2. Certificate of Death: Bertha Stroebele. Filed 28 January 1911. State of New Jersey, Bureau of Vital Statistics, Certificate of Record of Death, Reg. No. 9187. Informant: John J. Stroebele husband of deceased], Jersey City, New Jersey.

3. David Stroebel, "Re: "Records of Relative's Employment with Emperor Wilhelm I," email message to oeffentlichkeitsarbeit@senstadt.berlin.de, 31 December 2008.

4. Manchester, *Arms of Krupp*. 77.

5. Certificate of Death: Walburga Bertha Stroebele. Filed 5 November 1877. City of Sigmaringen, German State of Baden-Wurttemberg, City Registrar, Reg. No. 102. Informant: John Stroebele father of deceased], Sigmaringen, Baden-Wurttemberg, Germany. Bertha Stroebele SS *Westphalia* Passenger Manifest, 27 March 1883. Online database castlegarden.org. Passenger and Crew Lists of Vessels Arriving at New York, 1855 to 1890. Certificate of Death: John Stroebele. Filed 28 June 1930. State of New Jersey, Bureau of Vital Statistics, Certificate of Record of Death, Reg. No. 2969. Informant: Adolph Stroebele son of deceased], Jersey City, New Jersey.

6. German Death Record, Johann Stroebele. Freiberg Archives, Baden-Wurttemberg, Germany. 1 July 1948. Certificate of Death: Emma Kromer. Filed 23 December 1925. City of Sigmaringen, German state of Baden-Wurttemberg, City Registrar, Reg. No. 102. Informant: Eugene John Kromer, son of deceased, Sigmaringen, Baden-Wurttemberg, Germany.

Chapter 6

1. Manchester, *Arms of Krupp*. 182.

2. Manchester, *Arms of Krupp*. 204.

3. Manchester, *Arms of Krupp*. 194.

4. Manchester, *Arms of Krupp*. 182.

5. Manchester, *Arms of Krupp*. 182.

6. Manchester, *Arms of Krupp*. 182.

7. Manchester, *Arms of Krupp*. 182.

8. Manchester, *Arms of Krupp*. 182.

9. Certified transcription of birth certificate for John Joseph Stroebele Jr. 16 March 1876, Civil Registry Office of Sigmaringen, extract from birth registration.

10. Manchester, *Arms of Krupp*. 182.

11. Manchester, *Arms of Krupp*. 82.

12. Manchester, *Arms of Krupp*. 82.

13. Manchester, *Arms of Krupp*. 149.

14. Certificate of Death: Walburga Bertha Stroebele. Filed 5 November 1877. City of Sigmaringen, German state of Baden-Wurttemberg, City Registrar, Reg. No. 102. Informant: John Stroebele father of deceased], Sigmaringen, Baden-Wurttemberg, Germany.

15. Certificate of Death: Walburga Bertha Stroebele. Filed 5 November 1877. City of Sigmaringen, German state of Baden-Wurttemberg, City Registrar, Reg. No. 102. Informant: John Stroebele father of deceased], Sigmaringen, Baden-Wurttemberg.

16. Manchester, *Arms of Krupp.* 182.

17. Caroline Marchuck, telephone conversation with author, 18 September 2008.

18. Manchester, *Arms of Krupp,* 182.

Chapter 7

1. Manchester, *Arms of Krupp.* Back cover.

2. "Salute to the Stroebels," The *Jersey Journal,* 30 October 1942, 1.

3. Johann Stroebke, SS *Zeeland* Passenger Manifest, 5 December 1882. Online database castlegarden.org. Passenger and Crew Lists of Vessels Arriving at New York, 1855 to 1890.

4. Gjenvick Gjonvik Archives. "Second Cabin, Steerage and Regular Service of the Hamburg-American Line." Gjenvick Gjonvik Archives. gjenvick. com. 12 February 2009.

5. Norwegian Heritage. "Norwegian Heritage Hands Across the Sea." Norwegian Heritage. norwayheritage.com/p_shiplist.asp?co=natio. 12 February 2009.

6. Officer, L., and Williamson, S. 4 May 2004, from the measuring worth website, http://www.measuringworth.com.

7. Declaration of intention of John J. Stroebel, Declarations of Intention No. 1466, Clerk of the Court of Common Pleas of Hudson County, Jersey City, New Jersey.

8. Stroebele Charles M. Stroebele "Re: Sedan, France and Stroebele" email message to author, 31 December 2009.

9. Otto Stroebell, SS *Allemannia* Passenger Manifest, 11 June 1866. Online database castlegarden.org. Passenger and Crew Lists of Vessels Arriving at New York, 1855 to 1890.

10. City of Berlin. "Senate Department for Urban Development/Around the Royal Palace/View from Kaiser Wilhelm Bridge." stadtentwicklung.berlin.de/bauen/wanderungen/en/sch_09.shtml. 22 March 2009.

11. Josef Kugler, "Re: Kein Betreff," email message to author, 11 December 11, 2008.

12. Baptismal record for John Joseph Stroebele Baptismal Register, page unkn, Freiburg Archives, Baden-Wurttemberg, Germany.

13. Baptismal record for John Joseph Stroebele Baptismal Register, page unkn, Freiburg Archives, Baden-Wurttemberg, Germany.

14. *"Heights Pals on Sea Duty,"* Jersey Observer. 26 November 1940.

15. Manchester, *Arms of Krupp*, 194.

16. *"John J. Stroebele Sr. with Prussian Army medals."* Photograph. Albany, New York. January 1952.

17. Stroebele Charles M. Stroebele "Re: Sedan, France and Stroebele" email message to author, 31 December 2009.

18. ThyssenKrupp. "Alfried Krupp von Bohlen und Halbach Foundation Krupp Historical Archive, Archive history." thyssenkrupp.com/en/konzern/geschichte_archive_k1_2.html. 4 April 2009.

19. Letter, Alfried Krupp von Bohlen und Halbach-Stiftung, to author, August 25, 2009.

20. Hugo von Werden, photographer. *"Krupp Family with Friends," Pictures of Krupp: Photography and History in the Industrial age.* Photograph. Essen, Westphalia. Philip Wilson Publishers, 2005. 209.

21. Manchester, *Arms of Krupp*, 28.

22. Baptismal record for Arnold Krupp, Baptismal Register, Protestant Church of Essen.

23. Church of Jesus Christ of Ladder-day Saints, "Ancestral File," FamilySearch (online: Intellectual Reserve, Inc., 1999-2010), Individual Record of Lorenz STROEBELE (ancestral Batch Number: C04134-7), Source Film Number: 1050213. pilot.familysearch.org, accessed 13 July 2009.

24. Marriage record for John Stroebele and Engelbertha Arnold, 31 August 1875 St. John's Catholic Church Register, Sigmaringen, Baden-Wurttemberg, Germany.

25. State of Baden-Wurttemberg. "Emigration from Southwest-Germany." "Emigration from Southwest-Germany." auswanderer-bw.de/sixcms/detail.php?template=a_artikel&id=6591&. 17 May 2009.

Chapter 8

1. Obituary for Theodore "Ted" Stroebele Monticello, N.J. Times Herald-Record/Recordonline.com, 14 March 2005.

2. Obituary for Theodore "Ted" Stroebele Monticello N.J. Times Herald-Record/Recordonline.com, 14 March 2005.

3. Meeting minutes. "Regular Meeting of the Board of Trustees, Village of Monticello, N.Y." Monday, June 6, 2005.

4. Theodore J. Beebe Sr. telephone conversation with author, 18 July 2008.

5. Letter, Marie Kromer, to John Stroebele Sr. February 8, 1926.

6. Post card, Mortiz, to Aunt Josephine, Lottie and Uncle Fred, April 9, 1923.

7. Certificate of Death: Emma Kromer. Filed 23 December 1925. City of Sigmaringen, German state of Baden-Wurttemberg, City Registrar, Reg. No. 102. Informant: Eugene John Kromer, son of deceased], Sigmaringen, Baden-Wurttemberg.

8. Theodore J. Beebe Sr. telephone conversation with author, 28 October 2008. *Albany Directory for the Year Ending 1915*, Albany Public Library, 631.

9. Charles M. Stroebele telephone conversation with author, 28 October 2008.

10. US Army enlistment record, John J. Stroebele March 19, 1898. A.G.O. No. 11, December 7, 1895. National Archives and Records Administration, Washington, D.C.

11. Boyd's Jersey City and Hoboken Directory, (1895-97), 620.

12. 1910 U.S. Federal Census (population schedule), Jersey City, Hudson County, New Jersey, Dwelling 198, Family 94, John Stroebele household," jpeg image, (online: The Generations Network, Inc., 2001) [Digital scan of original records in the National Archives, Washington, DC], subscription database, <http://www.ancestry.com>, accessed 16 December 2009.

13. 1920 U.S. Federal Census (population schedule), Albany City, Albany County, New York, Dwelling 248, Family 286, John J. Stroebele household," jpeg image, (online: The Generations Network, Inc., 2001) [Digital scan of original records in the National Archives, Washington, DC], subscription database, <http://www.ancestry.com>, accessed 16 December 2009.

14. 1930 U.S. Federal Census (population schedule), Thompson Township, Sullivan County, New York, Dwelling 41, Family 41, John J. Stroebele household," jpeg image, (online: The Generations Network, Inc., 2001) [Digital scan of original records in the National Archives, Washington, DC], subscription database, <http://www.ancestry.com>, accessed 16 December 2009. Charles M. Stroebele telephone conversation with author, 17 October 2008.

15. Photograph, "John J. Stroebele Sr. John J. Stroebele Jr." January 1927.

16. Theodore J. Beebe Sr. telephone conversation with author, 28 October 2008.

17. Greg Harlow, telephone conversation with author, 5 May 2009.

18. Deed, Lena and Fred Ehling to John and Linda Stroebel, Albany County Deed Book 262, 390.

19. 1930 U.S. Federal Census (population schedule), Thompson Township, Sullivan County, New York, Dwelling 41, Family 41, John J. Stroebele household," jpeg image, (online: The Generations Network, Inc., 2001) [Digital scan of original records in the National Archives, Washington, DC], subscription database, <http://www.ancestry.com>, accessed 16 December 2009.

Chapter 9

1. WH. Boyd Gopsill (1883-84), Jersey City and Hoboken Directory, 436. Declaration of intention of John J. Stroebel, Declarations of Intention No. 1466, Clerk of the Court of Common Pleas of Hudson County, Jersey City, New Jersey.

2. Norwegian Heritage. "Hands Across the Sea" norwayheritage.com/p_ shiplist.asp?co=natio. (12 November 2009).

3. Adolph Stroebele SS *Hermann* Passenger Manifest, 22 October 1866. Online database castlegarden.org. Passenger and Crew Lists of Vessels Arriving at New York, 1855 to 1890.

4. Norwegian Heritage. "Hands Across the Sea" norwayheritage.com/p_ shiplist.asp?co=natio. (12 November 2009).

5. *Housing Conditions in Jersey City*, Mary Sayles, January, 1903, 49.

6. Officer, L., and Williamson, S. 4 May 2009, from the MeasuringWorth Website, http://www.measuringworth.com.

7. Officer, L., and Williamson, S. 4 May 2004, from the MeasuringWorth Website, http://www.measuringworth.com.

8. Commerzbank, "Re: Bank Record Inquiry for German Relative," email message to author, 15 May 2009.

9. Declaration of intention of John J. Stroebel, Declarations of Intention No. 1466, Clerk of the Court of Common Pleas of Hudson County, Jersey City, New Jersey.
Caroline Marchuck, telephone conversation with author, 18 September 2008.

10. Cynthia Harris, "Re: "Heights Elementary Schools," email message to author, 5 January 2009.

11. Ancestry.com, "World War I Draft Registration Cards 1917-1918 for Otto Stroebel" in Ancestry.com at http://search.ancestry.com/cgi-bin/sse.dll?gl=39&rank=1&new=1&so=3&MSAV=0&msT=1&gss=ms_f-39&gsfn=Otto&gsln=Stroebel&_81004010=1882&msbpn=3253&msbpn_PInfo=3-%7C1652381%7C3253%7C&msbpn__ftp=Germany&msrpn=8017&msrpn_PInfo=8-%7C1652393%7C2%7C3244%7C33%7C1411%7C8017%7C&msrpn__ftp=Jersey+City%2C+New+Jersey%2C+USA&uidh=e74 (accessed 23 January 2009). Original source: United States. Selective Service System. World War I Selective Service Draft Registration Cards 1917-1918, National Archives Microfilm Publications M1509, (Washington, D.C.: NARA, 1987-1988). !NAME-RESIDENCE: Otto Stroebel, Jersey City, Hudson, New Jersey.

12. Deed from Joseph E. Reilly and Helen Reilly to Otto and Julia Stroebel, 8 Feb 1928, Hudson County Deed Book 1673, 579, Registrar's Office, Jersey City, New Jersey.

13. Deed from Mortgage and Investment Company of New Jersey to Otto and Julia Stroebel, Hudson County Deed Book 1665, 451, Registrar's Office, Jersey City, New Jersey.

14. Deed from The Hoboken Building and Loan Association to Jefferson Trucking and Rigging Co., Inc., 31 Jul 1927, Hudson County Deed Book 1578, 180-1, Registrar's Office, Jersey City, New Jersey.

Chapter 10

1. Baptismal record for Otto William Stroebel, Baptismal Register, St. Paul of the Cross Roman Catholic Church, Jersey City, New Jersey.

2. 1920 U.S. Federal Census (population schedule), Albany City, Albany County, New York, Dwelling 248, Family 286, John J. Stroebele household," jpeg image, (online: The Generations Network, Inc., 2001) [Digital scan of original records in the National Archives, Washington, DC], subscription database, <http://www.ancestry.com>, accessed 16 December 2009.

3. *Sheet Metal Worker's Journal*, Jan 1922, 37.

4. *Albany Directory for the Year Ending 1915*, Albany Public Library, 631.

5. *Albany Directory for the Year Ending 1918*, Albany Public Library, 567.

6. Theodore J. Beebe Sr. telephone conversation with author, 9 July 2009.

7. "New York Passenger Lists, 1820-1957," John J. and Linda Stroebele" jpeg image, (Online: The Generations Network, Inc., 2001) [Digital scan of original records in the National Archives, Washington, DC], subscription database, <http://www.ancestry.com>, microfilm serial: T715_4363; Line: 9. accessed 12 June 2009.

8. Indenture from Carl Moog to John and Linda Stroebele Albany County Deed Book 409, 156.

9. Indenture from Adam and Helen Sobiecki to John and Linda Stroebele 11 Mar 1926, Deed Book 740, 238.

10. Deed from Carl Moog to John and Linda Stroebele Albany County Deed Book 227, 376, Registrar's Office, Albany, New York.

11. Theodore J. Beebe Sr. telephone conversation with author, 9 July 2009.

12. Charles M. Stroebele telephone conversation with author, 17 October 2008.

13. Charles M. Stroebele telephone conversation with author, 17 October 2008.

14. 1920 U.S. Federal Census (population schedule), Albany City, Albany County, New York, Dwelling 248, Family 286, John J. Stroebele household," jpeg image, (online: The Generations Network, Inc., 2001) [Digital scan of original records in the National Archives, Washington, DC], subscription database, <http://www.ancestry.com>, accessed 16 December 2009.

15. Ancestry.com, "World War I Draft Registration Cards 1917-1918." John Stroebele Jr." in Ancestry.com at http://search.ancestry.com/ cgi-bin/sse.dll?gl=39&rank=1&new=1&so=3&MSAV=0&mst=1&g ss=ms_r_f-39&gsfn=John&gsln=Stroebele&_81004010=1876&msb pn=3253&msbpn_PInfo=3-%7C1652381%7C3253%7C&msbpn__ ftp=Germany&msrpn=8014&msrpn_PInfo=8-%7C1652393%7C2%7 C3244%7C33%7C1411%7C8014%7C&msrpn__ftp=Hoboken%2C+N ew+Jersey%2C+USA&uidh=e74 (accessed 27 October 2008). Original source: United States. Selective Service System. World War I Selective Service Draft Registration Cards 1917-1918, National Archives Microfilm Publications M1509, (Washington, D.C.: NARA, 1987-1988). !NAME-RESIDENCE: John Stroebele Hoboken, Hudson, New Jersey.

16. Indenture, April 2, 1923, between Carl Moog and John and Linda Stroebele 55 Ontario Street, Albany, NY. Book 409, 156.

17. 1930 U.S. Federal Census (population schedule), Thompson Township, Sullivan County, New York, Dwelling 41, Family 41, John J. Stroebele household," jpeg image, (online: The Generations Network, Inc., 2001) [Digital scan of original records in the National Archives, Washington, DC], subscription database, <http://www.ancestry.com>, accessed 16 December 2009.

18. Theodore J. Beebe Sr. telephone conversation with author, 9 July 2009.

19. Indenture, April 2, 1923, between Carl Moog and John and Linda Stroebele 55 Ontario Street, Albany, NY. Book 409, 156.

20. Indenture, 2 Apr 1923, between Carl Moog and John and Linda Stroebele 55 Ontario Street, Albany, NY. Book 409, 156.

21. Deed from Henry Klob to John and Linda Stroebele Albany County Deed Book 692, 238, Registrar's Office, Albany, New York.

22. Deed from Carl Moog to John and Linda Stroebele Albany County Deed Book 227, 376, Registrar's Office, Albany, New York.

23. Mortgage from John and Linda Stroebele to Christina Bauch Fritschie, date, Albany County Mortgage Book 227, 201.

24. Mortgage $806.80, paid to Christina Bauch Fritschie, by John and Linda Stroebele for Edward Y. LeFevre, 11 Jan 1928, Albany County Mortgage Book n.a., 283.

25. Deed from Henry Klob to John and Linda Stroebele Albany County Deed Book 692, 238, Registrar's Office, Albany, New York.

26. Deed from Lena Ehling to John and Linda Stroebele Albany County Deed Book 262, 390.

27. Deed from Lena Ehling to John and Linda Stroebele Albany County Deed Book 262, 390.

28. Deed from Philip and Franziska Lowe to John and Linda Stroebele Albany County Deed Book n.a., 192, Registrar's Office, Albany, New York. Deed from Philip and Franziska Lowe to John and Linda Stroebele Albany County Deed Book unkn, 192, Registrar's Office, Albany, New York.

29. Deed from John and Linda Stroebele to Charles and June Stroebele 24 Aug 1959, Albany County Deed Book 1624, 59, Registrar's Office, Albany, New York.

30. Theodore J. Beebe Sr. telephone conversation with author, 27 April 2009.

31. "Josephine and Linda Stroebele." Photograph. Asbury Park, New Jersey. C. 1920.

32. Officer, L., and Williamson, S. 4 May 2009, from the MeasuringWorth Website, measuringworth.com.

33. Charles M. Stroebele telephone conversation with author, 2 April 2009.

34. Officer, L., and Williamson, S. 4 May 2009, from the Measuringworth Website, measuringworth.com.

35. Officer, L., and Williamson, S. 4 May 2009, from the MeasuringWorth Website, measuringworth.com.

36. "Josephine, Barbara and Florence Stroebele." Photograph. Albany, New York. C. 1920.

37. Officer, L., and Williamson, S. 4 May 2009, from the MeasuringWorth Website, measuringworth.com.

38. Charles M. Stroebele telephone conversation with author, 17 October 2008.

39. Charles M. Stroebele telephone conversation with author, 17 October 2008.

40. Charles M. Stroebele telephone conversation with author, 2 April 2009.

Chapter 11

1. Kate Woodbridge Michaelis, Ortho E. Michaelis, E. Monthaye, E. *Alfred Krupp: a sketch of his life and work: after the German of Victor Niemeyer*, 3.

2. 1900 U.S. Federal Census (population schedule), Jersey City, Hudson County, New Jersey, Dwelling 115, Family 155, John Stroebele household," jpeg image, (online: The Generations Network, Inc., 2001) [Digital scan of original records in the National Archives, Washington, DC], subscription database, <http://www.ancestry.com>, accessed 16 December 2009.

3. 1900 U.S. Federal Census (population schedule), Jersey City, Hudson County, New Jersey, Dwelling 115, Family 155, John Stroebele household," jpeg image, (online: The Generations Network, Inc., 2001) [Digital scan of original records in the National Archives, Washington, DC], subscription database, <http://www.ancestry.com>, accessed 16 December 2009.

4. Certificate of Death: Bertha Stroebele. Filed 28 January 1911. State of New Jersey, Bureau of Vital Statistics, Certificate of Record of Death, Reg. No. 9187. Informant: John J. Stroebele husband of deceased], Jersey City, New Jersey.

5. Bertha Stroebele SS *Westphalia* Passenger Manifest, 27 March 1883. Online database castlegarden.org. Passenger and Crew Lists of Vessels Arriving at New York, 1855 to 1890.

6. Certificate of Death: Bertha Stroebele. Filed 28 January 1911. State of New Jersey, Bureau of Vital Statistics, Certificate of Record of Death, Reg. No. 9187. Informant: John J. Stroebele husband of deceased], Jersey City, New Jersey.

7. 1910 U.S. Federal Census (population Schedule), Jersey City, Hudson County, New Jersey, Dwelling 198, Family 94, John Stroebele household," jpeg image, (online: The Generations Network, Inc., 2001) [Digital scan of original records in the National Archives, Washington, DC], subscription database, <http://www.ancestry.com>, accessed 16 December 2009.

8. 1930 U.S. Federal Census (population schedule), Jersey City, Hudson County, New Jersey, Dwelling 114, Family 183, Julia Stroebel household," jpeg image, (online: The Generations Network, Inc., 2001) [Digital scan of original records in the National Archives, Washington, DC], subscription database, <http://www.ancestry.com>, accessed 2 May 2009.

9. Stroebele Charles M. Stroebele "Re: Sedan, France and Stroebele" email message to author, 31 December 2009.

10. Manchester, *Arms of Krupp*, 209.

11. Certificate of Death: Bertha Stroebele. Filed 28 January 1911. State of New Jersey, Bureau of Vital Statistics, Certificate of Record of Death, Reg. No. 9187. Informant: John J. Stroebele husband of deceased], Jersey City, New Jersey.

12. Church of Jesus Christ of Ladder-day Saints, "Ancestral File," FamilySearch (online: Intellectual Reserve, Inc., 1999-2010). Individual Record of Lorenz Stroebele (ancestral batch number: C04134-7), Source Film Number: 1050213. pilot.familysearch.org, accessed 13 July 2009.

13. *Nature doctors: pioneers in naturopathic medicine*. Friedhelm Kirchfeld, Wade Boyle. Portland, OR. Medicina Biologica, East Palestine, Ohio. Buckeye Naturopathic Press, ©1994. 221.

Chapter 12

1. Church of Jesus Christ of Ladder-day Saints, "Ancestral File," Family-Search (online: Intellectual Reserve, Inc., 1999-2010), Individual Record of Konrad Stroebele (ancestral Batch Number: J945461), Source Call Number: 0912191. familysearch.org, accessed 15 July 2009.

2. "Krupp, the gunmaker, dies suddenly," The *New York Times*. November 22, 1902, 5.

3. Manchester, *Arms of Krupp*, 204-206.

4. Manchester, *Arms of Krupp*, 456-457.

5. Manchester, *Arms of Krupp*, 370, 384.

6. Manchester, *Arms of Krupp*, 9.

7. *The Overland Monthly*, Vol. LXXII- Second Series. July-December, 1918, 77.

8. Charles M. Stroebele "Re: Sedan, France and Stroebele" email message to author, 31 December 2009.

9. Certificate of Death: John Stroebele. Filed 28 June 1930. State of New Jersey, Bureau of Vital Statistics, Certificate of Record of Death, Reg. No. 2969. Informant: Adolph Stroebele [son of deceased], Jersey City, New Jersey.

10. U.S. Army, Enlistment Record: John J. Stroebele Jr. March 19, 1898. A.G.O. No. 11, December 7, 1895.

Chapter 13

1. German birth record for Emma Stroebele. Freiberg Archives, Baden-Wurttemberg. 7 September 1846.

2. Marriage record for Emma Stroebele and Eugene Kromer, 10 August 1869, St. John's Catholic Church Register, Sigmaringen, Baden-Wurttemberg, Germany.

3. Marriage record for Emma Stroebele and Eugene Kromer, 10 August 1869, St. John's Catholic Church Register, Sigmaringen, Baden-Wurttemberg, Germany.

4. Marriage record for Emma Stroebele and Eugene Kromer, 10 August 1869, St. John's Catholic Church Register, Sigmaringen, Baden-Wurttemberg, Germany.

5. Otto Stroebell, SS *Allemannia* Passenger Manifest, 11 June 1866. Passenger Manifest, 5 December 1882. Adolph Stroebele SS *Hermann* Passenger Manifest, 22 October 1866. Online database castlegarden.org. Passenger and Crew Lists of Vessels Arriving at New York, 1855 to 1890. Bertha Stroebele SS Westphalia Passenger Manifest, 27 March 1883. Online database castlegarden.org. Passenger and Crew Lists of Vessels Arriving at New York, 1855 to 1890.

6. Letter, Marie Kromer, to John Stroebele August 11, 1926.

7. "Emma, Eugene, Eugene John, Emma Anna, and Marie Emma Kromer." Photographs. Sigmaringen, Baden-Wurttemberg. n.d.

8. Kugler, G.F., Photographer. Emma Kromer 1878. Photograph. Sigmaringen, Baden-Wurttemberg, Germany. c.1878.

9. J.H. Smith, Photographer. "Emma Kromer 1892." Photograph. Newark, New Jersey. 1892.

10. Young, Sol. Photographer. "Emma Kromer 1906." Photograph. New York, New York. Sol Young Studios.

11. "Emma Kromer with John and Engelbertha Stroebele." Photograph. 25 November 1906.

12. Kugler, F. *"Emma Kromer 1914."* Photograph. Sigmaringen, Baden-Wurttemberg. F. Kugler Hofphotograph. c. 1914.

13. 1900 U.S. Federal Census (population schedule), Jersey City, Hudson County, New Jersey, Dwelling 115, Family 155, John Stroebele household," jpeg image, (online: The Generations Network, Inc., 2001) [Digital scan of original records in the National Archives, Washington, DC], subscription database, <http://www.ancestry.com>, accessed 18 December 2009.

14. "Wed 50 Years." *Albany-Times Union*, 20 October 1952. Marriage record for Lena Lamprecht and Adolph Stroebele 14 January 1902, Immaculate Conception Roman Catholic Church, Register No. 3461, Secaucus, New Jersey. Marriage record for Julia Hauser and Otto Stroebel, 12 September 1906, Our Lady of Grace Roman Catholic Church, Register No. 762, Hoboken, New Jersey.

Chapter 14

1. David Stroebel, "Re: Ahnenforschung," email message to Karl-Heinz Berger, 25 September 2009.

2. David Stroebel, "Re: Additional Krupp Family Photos," email message to Professor Rasch, 11 March 2009.

3. David Stroebel, "Re: Additional Krupp Family Photos," email message to Professor Rasch, 11 March 2009.

4. Letter, author to Villa Hugel, 10 April 2009.

5. Letter, "Permission to use Krupp photographs in book." Dr. Ralf Stremmel, Alfried Krupp von Bohlen und Halbach-Stiftung Historisches Archiv Krupp Villa Hugel to David Stroebel, September 30, 2008.

6. David Stroebel, "Re: Hugel Reply," email message to Dr. Ralf Stremmel, 13 April 2009.

7. Christa Brachvogel, "Re: Historisches Archiv Krupp," email message to author, 25 August 2009.

8. David Stroebel, "Re: Friedrich Krupp Baptism," email message to info@ev-kirche-kettwig.de, 20 April 2009.

9. Baptismal record for Friedrich Alfred Krupp, Baptismal Register, Protestant Church of Essen, Essen, North Rhine-Westphalia, Germany.

10. Baptismal record for Friedrich Alfred Krupp, Baptismal Register, Protestant Church of Essen, North Rhine-Westphalia, Germany.

11. Stefan Koppleman, "Re: Letter of 17 June 2009, Friedrich Krupp Birth Record," email message to author, 3 August 2009.

12. Stefan Koppleman, "AW: Information about you for book," email message to author, 12 August 2009.

13. Stefan Koppleman, "Re: Copy of Alfried and Bertha Krupp's marriage record and name of church," 14 August 2009.

14. Letter, David Stroebel, to German Churches, January 4, 2010.

15. Karl-Heinz Berger, "Re: Ahnenforschung," email message to author, 15 July 2009.

16. Letter, Marie Kromer, to John Stroebele Sr. February 8, 1926.

17. David Stroebel, "Re: St. Johann's Church in Sigmaringen," email message to Burgermeister Dr. Daniel Rapp, 1 September 2009. Burgermeister Dr. Daniel Rapp, "Re: Information from the Mayor of Sigmaringen," email message to author, 15 September 2009.

Chapter 15

1. Hugo von Werden, photographer. "Krupp Family with Friends." *Pictures of Krupp: Photography and History in the Industrial age.* Photograph. Essen, Westphalia. Philip Wilson Publishers, 2005, 209.

2. Fifield, Christopher (2005). *Max Bruch: His Life and Times.* The Boydell Press, Woodbridge, 192.

3. Christopher Fifield, "Re: Photo of Clara Bruch with Krupps," email message to author 21 August 2009.

4. Christopher Fifield, "Re: Photo of Clara Bruch with Krupps," email message to author 21 August 2009.

5. Christopher Fifield, "Re: Photo of Clara Bruch with Krupps," email message to author 21 August 2009.

6. Fifield, *Max Bruch: His Life and Times,* 33.

7. Fifield, *Max Bruch: His Life and Times,* 33.

8. "Clara Bruch." Photograph. Cologne, North Rhine-Westphalia, Germany. Max Bruch Archive. n.d.

9. Baptismal record for Friedrich Alfred Krupp, Baptismal Register, Protestant Church of Essen, North Rhine-Westphalia, Germany.

10. Thyssenkrupp. "Founding Families, Alfred Krupp." ThyssenKrupp. com. thyssenkrupp.com/en/konzern/geschichte_grfam_k2.html. 24 December 2009.

11. Manchester, *Arms of Krupp*, 102.

12. Tenfelde, *Pictures of Krupp*, 250.

13. Tenfelde, *Pictures of Krupp*, 250.

14. Tenfelde, *Pictures of Krupp*, 250.

15. Manchester, *Arms of Krupp*, 192.

Chapter 16

1. Caroline Marchuck, telephone conversation with author, 18 September 2008.

2. Bertha Stroebele SS *Westphalia* Passenger Manifest, 27 March 1883. Online database castlegarden.org. Passenger and Crew Lists of Vessels Arriving at New York, 1855 to 1890.

3. Theodore J. Beebe Sr. telephone conversation with author, 18 December 2009.

4. Caroline Marchuck, telephone conversation with author, 18 September 2008.

5. Caroline Marchuck, telephone conversation with author, 18 September 2008.

6. Bertha Stroebele SS *Westphalia* Passenger Manifest, 27 March 1883. Online database castlegarden.org. Passenger and Crew Lists of Vessels Arriving at New York, 1855 to 1890.

7. 1920 U.S. Federal Census (population schedule), Albany City, Albany County, New York, Dwelling 248, Family 286, John J. Stroebele household," jpeg image, (online: The Generations Network, Inc., 2001) [Digital scan of original records in the National Archives, Washington, DC], subscription database, <http://www.ancestry.com>, accessed 16 December 2009.

8. Gopsill (1883-84), Jersey City and Hoboken Directory, 436.

9. Beverly G. Kirby-McDonough and Marge Spille, "Re: The Joseph Briggs House," email message to NJHudson@Rootsweb.com, 22 December 2008.

10. Michael J. Burlingham, "Re: Louis Tiffany Story on NYTimes.com," email message to author. January 7, 2009.

11. Certified transcription of birth certificate for John Joseph Stroebele Jr. 16 March 1876, Civil Registry Office of Sigmaringen, extract from birth registration.

12. Certificate of Death: Walburga Bertha Stroebele. Filed 5 November 1877. City of Sigmaringen, German state of Baden-Wurttemberg, City Registrar, Reg. No. 102. Informant: John Stroebele father of deceased], Sigmaringen, Baden-Wurttemberg, Germany.

13. Marriage record for John Joseph Stroebele and Engelbertha Arnold, 31 August 1875, St. John's Catholic Church Register, Sigmaringen, Baden-Wurttemberg, Germany.

14. Otto William Stroebel, birth certificate, no. 587 (1915), New Jersey State Archives, Trenton, New Jersey.

15. State of Baden-Wurttemberg. "Emigration from Southwest-Germany." "Emigration from Southwest-Germany." auswanderer-bw.de/sixcms/detail.php?template=a_artikel&id=6591&. 17 May 2009.

16. Bertha Stroebele SS *Westphalia* Passenger Manifest, 27 March 1883. Online database castlegarden.org. Passenger and Crew Lists of Vessels Arriving at New York, 1855 to 1890.

17. Bertha Stroebele SS *Westphalia* Passenger Manifest, 27 March 1883. Online database castlegarden.org. Passenger and Crew Lists of Vessels Arriving at New York, 1855 to 1890.

18. Marriage record for Emma Stroebele 10 Aug 1869, St. John's Catholic Church, Sigmaringen, Baden-Wurttemberg, Germany.

19. Caroline Marchuck, telephone conversation with author, 18 September 2008.

20. Manchester, *Arms of Krupp*, 209.

21. Manchester, *Arms of Krupp*, 182.

22. Manchester, *Arms of Krupp*, 456-457.

23. Certificate of Death: John Stroebele. Filed 28 June 1930. State of New Jersey, Bureau of Vital Statistics, Certificate of Record of Death, Reg. No. 2969. Informant: Adolph Stroebele son of deceased], Jersey City, New Jersey.

24. Certificate of Death: Bertha Stroebele. Filed 28 January 1911. State of New Jersey, Bureau of Vital Statistics, Certificate of Record of Death, Reg. No. 9187. Informant: John J. Stroebele husband of deceased], Jersey City, New Jersey.

25. Church of Jesus Christ of Ladder-day Saints, "Ancestral File," FamilySearch (online: Intellectual Reserve, Inc., 1999-2010), Individual Record of Anton Stroebele (ancestral Batch Number: C96946-1), Source Film Number: film 1050221. pilot.familysearch.org, accessed 13 July 2009.

26. *The National cyclopedia of American biography, being the history*, vol. 32, 1967, 506.

27. Manchester, *Arms of Krupp*, 102.

28. Manchester, *Arms of Krupp*, 71.

29. Manchester, *Arms of Krupp*, 75.

30. Manchester, *Arms of Krupp*, 158.

31. Manchester, *Arms of Krupp*, 151.

32. Manchester, *Arms of Krupp*, 153.

33. Manchester, *Arms of Krupp*, 82.

34. Certified transcription of birth certificate for John Joseph Stroebele Jr. 16 March 1876, Civil Registry Office of Sigmaringen, extract from birth registration.

35. Marriage record for John and Engelbertha Stroebele 31 August 1875 St. John's Catholic Church, Sigmaringen, Baden-Wurttemberg, Germany.

36. 1910 U.S. Federal Census (population schedule), Jersey City, Hudson County, New Jersey, Dwelling 198, Family 94, John Stroebele household," jpeg image, (online: The Generations Network, Inc., 2001) [Digital scan of original records in the National Archives, Washington, DC], subscription database, <http://www.ancestry.com>, accessed 16 December 2009.

37. 1910 U.S. Federal Census (population schedule), Jersey City, Hudson County, New Jersey, Dwelling 198, Family 94, John Stroebele household," jpeg image, (online: The Generations Network, Inc., 2001) [Digital scan of original records in the National Archives, Washington, DC], subscription database, <http://www.ancestry.com>, accessed 16 December 2009.

BIBLIOGRAPHY

Manchester, William R., *The Arms of Krupp*: 1587 - 1968. (Boston: Little, Brown and Company, 1968).

Kate Woodbridge Michaelis, Ortho E. Michaelis, E. Monthaye, *Alfred Krupp: a sketch of his life and work: after the German of Victor Niemeyer*. (New York: Thomas Prosser & Son, 1888).

Friedrich Carl Georg Muller, *Krupp's steel works* (London: William Heinemann, 1898).

"Stamford School of Medicine, Stroke Prevention, Stroke Center. " *Stamford University of Medicine*. 2009. http://strokecenter.stanford.edu/guide/prevention.html.

U.S. Army, *Trial of the major war criminals before the International Military Tribunal, Nuremberg*. 14 November 1945-1 October 1946: Documents and other material in evidence, Volume 36.

U.S. Army. WD AGO Form 53-98, *US Army Record and Report of Separation Certificate of Service. Stroebel, Otto, D.* 4 August 1947.

SS *Zeeland* "Passenger Manifest list for Bertha Stroebele," *Online database castlegarden.org, Passenger and Crew Lists of Vessels Arriving at New York, 1855 to 1890*, 5 December 1882, http://www.castlegarden.org/quick_search_detail.php?p_id=6351531

SS *Zeeland* "Passenger Manifest list for Johann Stroebke," *Online database castlegarden.org, Passenger and Crew Lists of Vessels Arriving at New York, 1855 to 1890*, 5 December 1882, http://www.castlegarden.org/quick_search_detail.php?p_id=6326524

The Church of Jesus Christ of Ladder-day Saints. Film No. 896138. Title: "*Kirchenbuch*, 1661-1900."

Tenfelde, Klaus. "1." *Pictures of Krupp: Photography and History in the Industrial Age*. London: Philip Wilson, 1994. Print.

Thyssenkrupp.com, *"Alfried Krupp von Bohlen und Halbach Foundation Krupp Historical Archive -Archive History,"* thyssenkrupp.com/en/konzern/ge-schichte_archive_k1_2.html.

New Jersey. Hudson County. 1900 U.S. Federal Census. Population schedule. Roll T623_980; Page: 8A; Enumeration District: 167. (online: Ancestry.com, Inc., 2002). (digital scan of original records in the National Archives, Washington, DC).

New Jersey. Hudson County. *1910 U.S.* Federal Census. Population sched-ule, Roll T624_892; Page: 10B; Enumeration District: 210; Image: 971. (online: Ancestry.com, Inc., 2002). (digital scan of original records in the National Archives, Washington, DC).

New Jersey. Hudson County. 1930 U.S. Federal Census. Population schedule. Roll 1356; Page: 9B; Enumeration District: 178; Image: 688.0 (online: Ancestry.com, Inc., 2002). (digital scan of original records in the National Archives, Washington, DC).

"Boy Drowns on Sled," *Hudson Dispatch*. Jersey City Free Public Library, January 18, 1922.

Certificate of Death for William Stroebele filed 20 March 1922, State of New Jersey, Bureau of Vital Statistics, *Certificate of Record of Death*, Reg. No. 1123.

Deed from The Hoboken Building and Loan Association to Jefferson Trucking and Rigging Co., Inc., Hudson County Deed Book 1578, 180-1, Registrar's Office, Jersey City, New Jersey.

Death certificate for Otto W. Stroebel filed 7 November 1928, State of New Jersey, Bureau of Vital Statistics, *Certificate of Record of Death*, Reg. No. 1123.

New Jersey Supreme Court, Julia Stroebel, Petitioner, Defendant-in-*Certiorari vs. Jefferson Trucking and Rigging Company*, Respondent, Prosecutor-in-Certiorari.

Social Security Death Index, Ancestry.com [database on-line] Provo, UT, Original Data: Social Security Administration, *Social Security Death Index*, Master File. Social Security Administration.

Cornelius Burnham Harvey, *Genealogical History of Hudson and Bergen Counties, New Jersey*. (New Jersey Genealogy Publishing Co. New York, 1900).

Obituary, Emma Engelbrecht, *Asbury Park Press*, 30 May 1991.

WH H. Boyd Gopsill (1883-84), *Jersey City, and Hoboken Directory*.

Certificate of Death for Bertha Stroebele files 28 January 1911, State of New Jersey, Bureau of Vital *Statistics Certificate and Record of Death*, Reg. No. 9187.

German death record for Walburga Bertha Stroebele Nr. 102, filed 5 November 1877, St. John's Catholic Church.

Certificate of death for John Joseph Stroebele filed 28 June 1930. State of New Jersey, Bureau of Vital Statistics, *Certificate of Record of Death, Reg. No. 2969.*

German death record for John Stroebele 1 July 1848, Freiburg, Baden-Wurttemberg, Germany Archives.

Certificate of death for Emma Kromer filed 23 December 1925. City of Sigmaringen, Baden-Wurttemberg, City Registrar, Reg. No. 102.

Certified German transcription of birth certificate for John Joseph Stroebele Jr. *16 March 1876*, Civil Registry Office of Sigmaringen, extract from birth registration.

Salute to the Stroebels, The *Jersey Journal*, 30 October 1942.

SS *Zeeland* "Passenger Manifest list for Johann Stroebke," *Online database castlegarden.org, Passenger and Crew Lists of Vessels Arriving at New York, 1855 to 1890*, 5 December 1882, http://www.castlegarden.org/search_02.php?m_ship=&po_port=&p_first_name=johann&p_last_name=stroeb*&o_occ=&co_country=&province=&town=&m_arr_date_start=1882&m_arr_date_end=1882&submit.x=53&submit.y=14

"Second Cabin, Steerage and Regular Service of the Hamburg-American Line 1890." Gjenvick Gjonvik Archives. http://www.gjenvick.com/Historical-Brochures/Steamships-OceanLiners/ScandinavianAmericanLine/1917-Brochure/SecondCabinAccommodations.html#axzz2ZWh2W6qy.

"Hands Across the Sea," Norwegian Heritage. 12 November 2009. http://norwayheritage.com/p_shiplist.asp?co=natio.

Measuringworth.com. 4 May 2004. http://www.measuringworth.com.

City of Berlin. Senate Department for Urban Development/Around the Royal Palace/View from Kaiser Wilhelm Bridge. http://www.stadtentwicklung.berlin.de/bauen/wanderungen/en/sch_09.shtml.

German birth record for Johann Strobele. Freiburg, Baden-Wurttemberg, Germany, Archives.

"Heights Pals on Sea Duty," Jersey Observer, November 26, 1940.

"John J. Stroebele Sr. with Prussian Army medals." Photograph. Albany, New York. January 1952.

Thyssenkrupp.com, *"Alfried Krupp von Bohlen und Halbach Foundation Krupp Historical Archive -Archive history,"* thyssenkrupp.com/en/konzern/geschichte_archive_k1_2.html.

Von Werden, Hugo. *Krupp Family with Friends.* 15 Aug 2009. *Pictures of Krupp: photography and history in the industrial age.* Philip Wilson Publishers (2005).

German baptism record for Arnold Krupp Protestant Church of Essen.

German Baptism record for Lorenz Stroebele http://www.pilot.familysearch.org. Batch C04134-7, File number: 1050213.

Marriage record for John and Engelbertha Stroebele 30 August 1875. St. John's Catholic Church.

State of Baden-Wurttemberg. "Emigration from Southwest-Germany." "Emigration from Southwest-Germany." auswanderer-bw.de/sixcms/detail.php?template=a_artikel&id=6591&. 17 May 2009.

Obituary. Theodore Ted Stroebele." *Times Herald-Record* accessed via recordonline.com. 14 March 2005.

"Regular Meeting of the Board Of Trustees Village of Monticello, New York." 6 June 2005.

Letter, Marie Kromer, to John Stroebele Sr. February 8, 1926.

Mortiz. Postcard to Aunt Josephine, Lottie and Uncle Fred. 9 April 1923.

Albany Directory for the Year Ending 1915, Albany Public Library, 631.

US Army enlistment record. John J. Stroebele. 19 March 1898. A.G.O. No. 11. 7 December 1895. National Archives and Records Administration, Washington, D.C.

W.H. H. Boyd Gopsill (1883-84), Jersey City, and Hoboken Directory, 436.

W. Andrew Boyd (1895-97), Jersey City and Hoboken Directory, 620.

New York. Albany County. 1920 U.S. Federal Census. Population schedule. Roll T625_1082; Page: 16B; Enumeration District: 91; Image: 916. (online: Ancestry.com, Inc., 2002). (digital scan of original records in the National Archives, Washington, DC).

New York. Sullivan County. 1930 U.S. Federal Census. Population schedule. Roll 1653; Page: 2A; Enumeration District: 38; Image: 598.0. (online: Ancestry.com, Inc., 2002). (digital scan of original records in the National Archives, Washington, DC).

Photograph, "John J. Stroebele Sr. John J. Stroebele Jr." January 1927.

Albany, County of. Registry of Deeds. Book 262, 390. 24 August 1959.

Norwegian Heritage. Hands Across the Sea. http://www.norwayheritage. com/p_shiplist.asp?co=natio.

Mary Siles, *Housing Conditions in Jersey City*. (College Settlements Association, 1903).

Officer, L., and Williamson, S. 4 May 2004, from the MeasuringWorth Website, http://www.measuringworth.com.

Declaration of intention of John J. Stroebel, No. 1466, Clerk of the Court of Common Pleas of Hudson County, Jersey City, New Jersey.

Hudson, County of. Registry of Deeds. Book 1673, 579. 8 February 1928.

Hudson, County of. Registry of Deeds. Book 1665, 451. 28 November 1927.

Hudson, County of. Registry of Deeds. Book 1578, 180. 8 February 1928. 31 July 1925.

Baptismal record for Otto William Stroebel Jr. St. Paul of the Cross Catholic Church, Jersey City, New Jersey.

Amalgamated Sheet Metal Worker's Journal. Jan 1922, 37.

Albany Directory for the Year Ending 1915, Albany Public Library, 631.

Albany Directory for the Year Ending 1915, Albany Public Library, 567.

New York Passenger Lists. 1820-1957. microfilm serial: T715_4363. Ancestry.com. Line 9.

Albany, County of. Registry of Deeds. Book 409, 156. 2 April 1923.

Albany, County of. Registry of Deeds. Book 740, 238. 11 March 1826.

Albany, County of. Registry of Deeds. Book 227, 376. 13 June 1925.

Albany, County of. Registry of Deeds. Book 692, 238.

Albany, County of. Registry of Deeds. Book 227, 376. 13 June 1925.

Albany, County of. Registry of Mortgages. Book 229, 201.

Albany, County of. Registry of Mortgages. Book n.a. 283.

Sullivan, County of. Registry of Deeds. Book 262, 390.

Albany, County of. Registry of Deeds. Book n.a. 183. 21 October 1943.

Albany, County of. Registry of Deeds. Book n.a. 192. 4 January 1944.

Albany, County of. Registry of Mortgages. Book n.a. 192. 4 January 1944.

Albany, County of. Registry of Deeds. Book 1624, 59. 24 August 1959.

"Florence, Josephine and Linda Stroebele." Photograph. c.1922.

Warren R. Stroebel. Photograph. Gloria and Peter O. E. Bekker Sr. October 1942.

Friedhelm Kirchfeld, and Wade Boyle. *Nature doctors: pioneers in naturopathic medicine.* (Ohio: Buckeye Naturopathic Press 1994). 221.

Baptism record for Konrad Stroebele http://www.pilot.familysearch.org. International Genealogical Index, Batch No. J945461. Source Call No. 0912191.

"Krupp, the gunmaker, dies suddenly," The *New York Times.* 22 November 1902.

The Overland Monthly, Vol. LXXII- Second Series. July-December, 1918, 77.

US Army enlistment record, John J. Stroebele 19 March 1898. A.G.O. No. 11. 7 December 1895. National Archives and Records Administration.

German birth record for Emma Stroebel, Freiberg Archives, Baden-Wurttemberg, Germany.

Kugler, Joseph, Photographer. "Emma Kromer 1878." Photograph. Sigmaringen, Baden-Wurttemberg, Germany. c. 1878.

Smith, J.H., Photographer. "Emma Kromer 1892." Photograph. Newark, New Jersey. c. 1892.

Young, Sol. Photographer. "Emma Kromer 1906." Photograph. New York City, New York. c. 1906.

Kugler, F. Photographer. "Emma Kromer 1914." Photograph. Sigmaringen, Baden-Wurttemberg, Germany. c. 1914.

Photograph. "Emma Kromer with John and Engelbertha Stroebele." Photograph. Jersey City, New Jersey. 25 November 1906.

"Wed 50 Years," Albany-Times Union, 20 October 1952.

Adolph Theodore Stroebele and Lena Lamprecht, New Jersey Marriage Return No. 3461, Hudson County Register Office, Jersey City, New Jersey.

Otto Stroebel and Julia A. Hauser, New Jersey Marriage Return No. 762, Hudson County Register Office, Jersey City, New Jersey.

German birth record for Friedrich Alfred Krupp, Protestant Church of Essen, North Rhine-Westphalia, Germany.

David Stroebel, letter to German Churches, 4 January 2010.

Fifield, Christopher. Max Bruch: His Life and Times. The Boydell Press, Woodbridge, 2005.

"John J. Stroebele Sr. with Prussian Army medals." Photograph. Albany, New York. January 1952.

"Photograph of Clara Bruch." Photograph. Max Bruch Archiv, Musikwissenschaftliches Institut, Albertus-Magnus-Platz, Koln, Germany.

German Death Record, Walburga Bertha Strobele, Freiburg, Baden-Wurttemberg, Germany, Archives.

Birth certificate, Otto William Stroebel, New Jersey State Archives, Trenton, New Jersey.

State of Baden-Wurttemberg. "Emigration from Southwest-Germany." auswanderer-bw.de/sixcms/detail.php?template=a_artikel&id=6591&sprache=en&PHPSESSID=. 4 January 2009.

Baptismal record for Anton Stroebele http://www.pilot.familysearch.org. Batch C96946-1, film 1050221.

The National cyclopedia of American biography, being the history, vol. 32, 1967.

PICTURE CREDITS

Krupp Family with Friends	Krupp Archives, Essen
The real Clara Bruch	Max Bruch Archives, Cologne
Clara Bruch	Max Bruch Archives, Cologne, GE
Friedrich, Alfred, and Bertha Krupp	Krupp Archives, Essen
Alfred Krupp c. 1855	Krupp Archives, Essen
Big Bertha Howitzer	Krupp Archives, Essen
U-boat SM U-1	Wikimedia Commons
Bertha Krupp, nee Eichhoff	Krupp Archives, Essen
Friedrich Alfred "Fritz" Krupp	Wikimedia Commons

Bertha Krupp with son Friedrich	Krupp Archives, Essen
Villa Hugel- The Krupp Estate	Wikimedia Commona
Gustav Krupp von Bohlen und Halbach	Wikimedia Commons
Emperor Wilhelm I	Wikimedia Commons
Royal City Palace c.1900	Wikimedia Commons
Emperor Wilhelm II	Wikimedia Commons
St. John's Catholic Church	Sigmaringen.de
Castle Garden Immigration Center	Wikimedia Commons
356 Palisade Avenue	John Hallanan, President, Jersey City Landmarks Conservancy
Engelbertha Krupp	Charles M.
Stroebele c.1906	Stroebele
Emma, John and Engelbertha	Charles M.
Stroebele c.1906	Stroebele
Emma Stroebele Kromer 1878	Charles M. Stroebele
Emma Stroebele Kromer 1885	Charles M. Stroebele
Emma Stroebele Kromer 1892	Charles M. Stroebele

Emma and Marie Kromer 1914   Charles M. Stroebele

John Stroebele Jr. with
John Stroebel Sr. c.1926   Theodore J. Beebe Sr.

John Stroebele Jr. with wife
Linda Barbara Stroebele   Theodore J. Beebe Sr.

Caroline Marchuck   David G. Stroebel

Bertha Stroebele 1911 Death
Certificate   New Jersey State Archives

Theodore J. Beebe and Family   Theodore J. Beebe

Gloria and Peter O.E. Bekker Sr.   Peter O.E. Bekker Jr.

INDEX

Stroebel, Otto and Julia, deed for 353 Webster Avenue, 125

Stroebel, Otto and Julia, evidence of deed in Hudson County Clerk's Office, 125

Stroebel, Otto and Julia, Jefferson Trucking and Rigging, 31

Stroebel, Otto W., death of, 32

Stroebel, Otto W., knowledge of being the grandson of Bertha and Alfred Krupp, 151

Stroebel, Otto, 14, 181

Stroebel, Otto, employed by R. Doughty, 124

Stroebel, Otto, middle name given to honor Emperor Wilhelm I, 181

Stroebel, Otto, W., a third owner of Jefferson Trucking and Rigging Co., Inc., 124

Stroebel, Robert, death of, 24

Stroebel, Roland, stories of growing-up with financial difficulties, 135

Stroebel, US Army First Lieutenant Otto "Dave" 13

Stroebel, William Joseph, Emperor Wilhelm I, name passed to, 182

Stroebele Grill, 68, 70, 133, 136

Stroebele Grill, closure during prohibition, 130

Stroebele Adolph, 32, 34, 177, 178

Stroebele Adolph, baptism of in Sigmaringen, 181

Stroebele Adolph, bitter enemies with Julia Anne Stroebel, 33

Stroebele Adolph, brother of John Stroebele Sr. 119

Stroebele Adolph, brother of John, Sr. and Otto C. Stroebele 60

Stroebele Adolph, business partners with Otto W. Stroebel, 31

Stroebele Adolph, celebrated 7th birthday on day of immigration to US, 124

Stroebele Adolph, date of death, 154

Stroebele Adolph, finding children of, 27

Stroebele Adolph, Jefferson trucking and Rigging Company, Inc., 27

Stroebele Adolph, story of Engel-bertha Krupp marriage to John Stroebele passed down to Caroline Marchuck, 21

Stroebele Aloysia, daughter to Joseph Stroebele 186

Stroebele Aloysia, naturopathic medicine pioneer, 147

Stroebele Anton, 63, 64

Stroebele Anton, grandfather to John Stroebele Sr. 183

Stroebele Anton, marriage to Barbara Biedermann, 186

Stroebele Bertha, 28

Stroebele Charles, 158, 177, 178

ABOUT THE AUTHOR

David Stroebel began writing in 1992 when he became an Enlisted Air Force Reserve Command Field Historian at the 514th Air Mobility Wing at McGuire Air Force Base, New Jersey. He wrote extensively on the air and ground operations of various Air Force fighter and airlift wings. He also served with distinction as an Air Force Reserve Command First Sergeant. He is a 1992 political science graduate of William Paterson University in Wayne, New Jersey. He is married with three children and resides in Monmouth County, New Jersey.

Made in the USA
Columbia, SC
28 March 2018